The KitchenTable Method

From solo creative to agency owner

John Ashton

Write Arm.

First published in 2019 by
Write Arm
7 Marlborough Place
Brighton
BN2 1HP
United Kingdom

ISBN-978-1-5272-4657-7

British Library Cataloguing-in-Publication Data
A catalogue record for this book is available from the British Library

Design by Buckley Creative
www.buckleycreative.co.uk

Cover photography by Richard Hanson
www.hansonimages.net

Contents

Introduction: What's the story?

No, not the guy from Beverley Hills Cop

Google 'John Ashton' and the first person to appear on the results page will be the American actor best known for his role in *Beverley Hills Cop*. Next will be the UK's former UN ambassador for climate change.

Keep scrolling down and you'll come to the head of public health in northwest England followed by the guitarist from the eighties band The Psychedelic Furs (you mean you've forgotten *Pretty in Pink*?).

Way down the list lurks a John Ashton whose meagre achievement of note is to have written three – yes, three – books about the Lockerbie disaster. That John Ashton is me.

My albatross

The Lockerbie story became my professional obsession. Having followed the case during my career in TV journalism, I ended up working for the lawyers of the man who was convicted of the bombing. I'd long believed Libyan Abdelbaset al-Megrahi to be innocent and the ongoing work fascinated me: it was my chance to make a difference and maybe, just maybe, to change history in a very modest way.

And yet, like many obsessions, Lockerbie soon became an albatross. As I was writing my biggest book on the case, I asked myself, 'What next?' Up to that point my career had been a series of unplanned happy accidents. I had fallen into my TV career and stumbled blindly into writing and legal research. I had trusted life to take me on a pleasant course and, till then, that trust had been rewarded.

But things had to change. I was no longer young. Employers were certainly not crying out for Lockerbie experts and journalism as a profession had been decimated by the growth of free online content.

So, what next? I needed a good plan to avoid ending up among the ever-growing pile of washed up media monkeys. I needed to earn well and I wanted a job that was flexible enough to allow me to spend time with my increasingly frail mother, who lived 200 miles and four train journeys away.

No more media monkey or frantic freelancer

I knew that I wanted a fresh challenge. But what? I had enjoyed freelancing as a commercial writer a couple of years earlier. The idea of going back to that seemed sensible, but not particularly appealing.

In order to make a good living as a freelancer I'd have to

work the same hours that I put in for staff jobs. Sure, I could take the odd morning off, but only if I put in an extra evening shift. More importantly, I wasn't convinced I could simply keep chasing commission after commission and call it a career.

That's when the idea of setting up a commercial writing agency came to me. As I saw it, it would give me more flexibility, would make life more interesting and might make me more money. Yet the thought of running a business with an office and staff just didn't appeal. To be frank, it seemed like too much responsibility for someone who craved freedom.

Fortunately though, history was on my side.

The digital surf's up – let's ride that wave

If you're over 35, you may just have noticed that the world has changed over the past couple of decades. You've probably noticed it the way that you would if you grew an extra head or relocated to the moon.

The digital revolution has affected almost every area of our lives. The effects are sometimes wonderful, occasionally terrifying and seldom less than dizzying. For me the greatest change that digital technology has enabled is not in how we buy, or how we learn, or even in how we exchange insults with strangers. It's in how we work.

For millions it has enabled a working lifestyle that only a couple of decades ago was an unobtainable fantasy. All that we now need in order to work is a computer and an internet connection. Commuting, wearing a suit, unpleasant colleagues and awkward situations the morning after office parties, can all be consigned to the dustbin marked *Thank God all that's behind me.*

All that we now need in order to work is a computer and an internet connection.

The biggest and most significant item in the dustbin is the office. Now we can connect to colleagues and clients online, be they in the next street, or on the other side of the world. It's the golden age of the creative freelancer and it has spawned a whole new subspecies, the digital nomad. Working for a client in Beijing from a guest house in the Andes is no longer a novelty.

But technology hasn't only liberated freelancers. It has also allowed many new business models – ones similarly unconstrained by geography or bricks and mortar.

Enter the KitchenTable agency

One day while sitting on a train in Glasgow I had my eureka moment. I wouldn't go back to being a freelance writer and I wouldn't set up a bricks and mortar agency. Instead I would take advantage of the digital revolution and set up a virtual agency that would use some of the great freelance writers I knew at its base.

This book is about that very model – a creative agency that utilises remote-working freelancers. I call it the KitchenTable agency, because you can run it from your kitchen table, although you could equally well run it from your back bedroom, your garden shed, or your AA meeting.

It's a model I chose because I wanted the lifestyle benefits of being freelance without all the hard grind. I also wanted to grow a business without being permanently tied to my desk and on the verge of burnout.

By the time I set up my agency, Write Arm, a couple of

years after that train journey, it still seemed like a great idea. The only snag was that I had no idea how to make it work. But I decided to do it anyway.

By then, in the spring of 2012, the pressure was really on. I had a nine-month-old son and my wife had taken redundancy and needed time to be a mother and plan her next career move. I also wanted to spend a lot of time with our son – there's nothing to beat the warm feeling that you get when your baby pisses on you.

I badly needed to earn and desperately hoped that Write Arm would deliver the goods – or rather the cash. It did. Within a few years, turnover grew from nothing to £500,000. Somehow, I had become a successful small businessman.

That's my story. What's yours?

If you're reading this then it's likely that you want to make a similar career shift to mine. You might be a copywriter like me, or you might be a designer, a web developer, a video maker, digital marketer, a photographer, an illustrator or one of the multitude of other creative professions.

Whatever your skillset, it's likely that we have some motivators in common. No doubt, you'll have some different ones too: perhaps you've fallen out of love with your profession, or you want to do a round-the-world trip (yes, you can do it if you run your own agency), or you're a power-crazed lunatic who likes the idea of bossing around a bunch of freelancers.

Whatever it is that is driving you, you need a roadmap. This book provides it – and I wish I'd had it back in 2012. It isn't the story of how I did it – not primarily, at least – although it is based on the knowledge that I accumulated on my journey.

Rather, it's a handbook for you to build your own KitchenTable agency and to do it quicker and better than I did. Sometimes my methodology is quite prescriptive and at other times it's fairly loose: this is friendly advice and handholding, rather than a formal coaching programme or a detailed financial blueprint.

Although my experience is of running a writing agency, the advice I offer can be applied to all types of KitchenTable agencies. That said, if you set up your own agency, it is likely to differ significantly from mine, not only in the type of services you offer, but also in the personality that you stamp upon it.

If you have bought this book, the chances are you're hungry for change. I hope it inspires you to take the plunge and set up your own KitchenTable agency. You won't regret it.

WHAT'S A KITCHENTABLE AGENCY

A KITCHENTABLE AGENCY MAINLY – OR EXCLUSIVELY – USES REMOTE-WORKING FREELANCERS TO PRODUCE ITS CREATIVE OUTPUT. YOU MAY PRODUCE SOME OF THE OUTPUT YOURSELF, BUT ONCE YOUR AGENCY IS WELL-ESTABLISHED YOU'LL PROBABLY WANT TO CONCENTRATE ON GROWING THE BUSINESS.

IF ALL OF YOUR AGENCY'S OUTPUT IS PRODUCED BY SALARIED STAFF, THEN IT'S NOT REALLY A KITCHENTABLE AGENCY. NOT THAT YOU SHOULDN'T EMPLOY SALARIED STAFF TO HELP YOU RUN THE COMPANY, THEY JUST SHOULDN'T BE DOING THE BULK OF THE CLIENT WORK.

WHATEVER FORM YOUR AGENCY TAKES AND WHATEVER IT PRODUCES, AT ITS HEART IS THE RECOGNITION THAT REMOTE, FLEXIBLE IS GOOD FOR ALL CONCERNED – FOR YOU, YOUR CLIENTS AND YOUR EMPLOYEES.

LEG
ONE

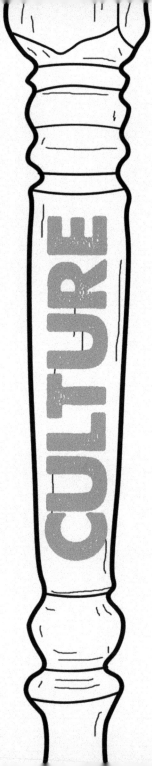

CULTURE

1 The foundations of company culture

I know what you're thinking: 'Culture? What kind of flaky crap are you about to feed us? We want to know how to run a business, not put on a play for our non-existent staff.' OK, I hear you, but listen: this might be the shortest section of the book, but it's actually the most important.

Your culture is your foundations

If done properly, culture is your biggest single asset. Like Red Bull, it gives you wings* – wings to lift you above your competitors and place you in the laps of clients. And, unlike Red Bull, if you mix it with vodka it doesn't make you dance all night and wake up feeling like you've been hit by a tank.

Culture isn't about the arts, although it is central to the art

*Fact of the day: Red Bull dropped its slogan, *Red Bull gives you wings* after being sued for 'false and deceptive advertising'.

of running a successful business. Culture is what gives you identity – and identity is central to your value. It's one of the main reasons that clients will want to hire you and freelancers will want to work for you.

Culture is your foundations. Get it right and you can build something wonderful. Get it wrong and, to switch metaphors, you could be heading for the cliffs faster than a lemming in a Maserati. Ignore it and the lemming will swap the Maserati for a tortoise – it will still reach the cliffs, only more slowly.

But how can you build a culture when you don't have any staff and everyone you employ works remotely? The answer is simple: you home in on the values and desires that are driving you, and project them into everything you do. Put them on your website and in your pitches, share them at networking events, tattoo them on to your forehead and, most importantly, live them.

Culture is your foundations. Get it right and you can build something wonderful

A brush with mortality

Where do you start with culture? You start inside your own head – and in my case what was going on was an electrical storm.

Let me explain. I was standing in a shop queue when I started to get very dizzy. I thought the feeling would pass, but it got worse. And then it all got a bit weird.

I started hearing voices in my head. Someone was singing a

song I knew well, but try as I might, I couldn't remember its name. Then the voice of the man behind me started coming through the mouth of the shopkeeper and vice versa. Then reality disappeared altogether.

When I woke up about 10 minutes later, I was in an ambulance being taken to hospital. The doctors examining me kept asking if I had bitten my tongue. I was fairly sure that I hadn't. They reckoned that I had probably fainted and let me go home. While I was in the cab back home my tongue began to throb. I had bitten it after all – it had just taken a while for the bruising to manifest.

The next day I visited the shop and asked the staff what had happened. They didn't speak great English, but they didn't need to: "You were really bad" said it all. They described how I had let out a big groan before crashing to the floor and shaking. I knew what it all meant. I hadn't fainted: I'd had a seizure.

Of course, I went straight on to Google to try to work out what it all meant. I soon discovered that the fit could have been caused by a brain tumour or a nasty underlying neurological condition. There were other, less sinister, explanations, but of course I feared the worst.

My doctor arranged for me to have a brain scan, but there was a two-month waiting list. When the day finally came, I was braced for very bad news. But, I'd have to wait - I had assumed that my neurologist would be on hand to interpret the results, but I was told there would be at least another month's wait for that.

The next day in desperation I called the neurologist's secretary and pleaded for the appointment to be brought forward. She said that wouldn't be possible, then capitulated and said she would have a word with the specialist. She returned to the phone a couple of minutes later and casually delivered the most important news I've ever had: 'Dr Nisbet has just looked at the scans and they are all clear.'

I was elated. I didn't have a brain tumour or a neuro-degenerative disease, I was merely epileptic.* To many that would have been a major blow, but to me it was a blessing. Sure, I would probably be on medication for life, but at least that life wasn't destined to end any time soon.

The big question

Why on earth am I telling you all this? It will all make sense shortly.

My life was not destined to end soon, but it did need to change radically. The fact is, you can only build an authentic and durable company culture by recognising and developing your own internal culture. You then wear that culture inside out – meaning that you put your personal priorities and values at the heart of your business.

In order to do all this, you have to start with a simple question, one that you dodge at your peril. If you avoid it, in a couple of years' time you might find yourself slumped over a bar on your tenth vodka and Red Bull, trying to figure out where it all went wrong.

The question is *Why?* Why am I starting a KitchenTable agency? Or, to put it another way, what is it I really want from life and how will setting up a KitchenTable agency help me to get it? You have to ask the question because the foundations of your company's culture must be your own needs and desires.

Which takes us back to my epilepsy. From the moment I was diagnosed, my priority was to look after myself. I

---

*A large proportion of epilepsy cases are, like mine, idiopathic, i.e. they have no known cause.

couldn't do that if I was commuting to someone else's office to work a 9-to-5 job. It would take too much of my day, would be stressful and wouldn't allow me enough time for rest, exercise and all of the other things that I needed to stay well. I needed freedom from demanding bosses and the work-a-day routine, and I needed work that would pay me money to not have to work at all hours.

So, my needs were pretty clear. What about my desires?

The foundations of your company's culture must be your own needs and desires.

What do you want?

What did I really want? The answer was simple: contentment.* I say simple, but the truth is that it was *so* simple that it eluded me for some time.

I imagine that, if you take time to explore your desires, contentment will probably be your answer too. But, having got this answer you have to really think: 'What makes me content?'

When I stopped to address this question, I was shocked that I had never really considered it before. It's such a basic desire yet it gets so easily drowned out by petty ones. The truth is that many people are more likely to ponder the Higgs Boson theory or how Donald Trump combs his hair than consider what actually makes them content. When I asked

---

*I say contentment rather than happiness as periodic unhappiness is a fact of life – one that the truly content can accommodate.

myself what made me content, the answers were relatively straightforward:

1. Work that I enjoyed
2. A good family life, including plenty of time with my children
3. The freedom to explore ideas, places and other work options
4. A good income
5. Plenty of human contact
6. But plenty of time to myself too.

The truth is that many people are more likely to ponder the Higgs Bosun theory or how Donald Trump combs his hair than consider what actually makes them content.

Your answers might be similar to mine, but maybe you would throw into the mix things like travelling the world or qualifying as a professional wrestler.

The four Fs

Whatever is on your list, it must include the first item in the list above. Having work that you enjoy is not only an end in itself, but it will also enable everything else on your list. The reason is simple: if you enjoy your work, you'll be good at it – and, if you're good at it, you'll make money. In my case enjoying myself and making money enabled the great family life that I wanted. In yours it might mean that you can go travelling or enroll on that wrestling course.

Having worked out the things that made me content and the centrality of work to that, I had to drill down further and ask myself what I needed from work to make it enjoyable.

I'm a slow learner and it took a while to find the answers again, even though, once more, they were fairly obvious. There were four of them and, conveniently, they all began with F.

Firstly, work had to be Fun.

I don't mean by that that I needed to come into work dressed as a clown (though, I generally do on Mondays and Wednesdays) or that I expected everyone I employed to be standup comedians. What it did mean was doing interesting work and working with interesting, friendly, sparky people. Of course, not every job is interesting and not everyone can be permanently interesting, friendly and sparky, but, as long as most were, work would be fun.

The second and third Fs were Freedom and Flexibility.

These Siamese twins are inextricably linked, both to each other and the second and third items on my original contentment list. The work had to give me the flexibility to spend time with my family when I needed to, including my elderly mother and my in-laws who lived in Germany. Flexibility also meant giving me the freedom to explore ideas, the world and other work projects.

All of this meant that I needed to be free from a desk, so I could work from wherever I needed to be and not tied down to a 9-to-5 routine.

The final F was less obvious: it was Fairness.

We don't usually consider fairness in our working lives until things go wrong. Things like having a bullying boss, or disloyal colleagues, or being overlooked for promotion, or being chosen for all the crap jobs.

Unfairness is like nasal hair – you can't be rid of it entirely, but you can keep it to a minimum. Keeping it to a minimum is all the easier when you're your own boss. And that's what I intended to do.

So, now I had four personal aims for my work that would form the backbone of my company culture: Fun, Freedom, Flexibility and Fairness. Next I had to wear those values inside out.

*In fact, a few of the freelancers I employ do stand-up comedy.

CHAPTER

2 | Building your company culture

Once you've established your own internal culture, building a company culture is fairly simple. As I said in the last chapter, it's about wearing your values inside out.

What do I mean by that? It's simple. It means that what you wish for yourself, you should wish for both your clients and employees. You should give clients and employees equal weight, because if your culture is to be authentic and durable it must face both ways.

The four Fs for clients

Let's consider clients first. How would those four Fs – Fun, Freedom, Flexibility and Fairness – apply to them?

Fun

It's not a word that clients would normally associate with working with a creative agency. Compared to a fortnight in Ibiza or an Eddie Izzard gig, commissioning an agency isn't up there as the most fun way to spend your time. I wasn't about to change that, but I could at least make working with my agency, Write Arm, enjoyable.

First and foremost, of course, that meant delivering great work to deadline, but it required far more. I made it a rule that every exchange I had with them, whether a meeting, call, email or text message, should be warm, friendly and positive.

Do such things really matter? Yes, they do. They really do. Put yourself in the shoes of an account manager or head of marketing who regularly commissions your services. Of course, they want your work to be great, but at a basic personal level they want their working day to be great too. If that day is punctuated by exchanges with people who are cold and negative, then it loses its shine.

If another supplier comes along who does equally good work for the same price, but is friendly and upbeat, then your client could suddenly be an ex-client. If your default setting is to be a miserable git, then paint on a smile. It will do wonders for your business and, who knows, it might even make you feel better.

Freedom

At the core of your client offering is that you free them from the hassle of managing multiple freelancers. What other freedoms can you offer? One of the other reasons that clients liked working with my agency is that we didn't tie them in to retainers.

There's another important freedom that you should offer clients – freedom from pestering. I pitched Write Arm, as a here-when-you-need-us, gone-when-you-don't service. I never got on our clients' backs trying to up-sell and cross-sell, and they respected me for it. Not that you shouldn't contact your clients if you have a new service or technology that might help their business, but before you pick up the phone ask yourself, 'Will they thank me for this?'

Flexibility

Once more the proposition for clients is as simple as it is attractive: they get the talent that they need when they need it. You might think that this is an offer too far for your agency, but you should really try to make it part of your service – your clients will love you for it.

If your default setting is to be a miserable git, then paint on a smile. It will do wonders for your business and, who knows, it might even make you feel better.

Fairness

That's simple: don't overcharge, don't underdeliver and don't try to blame them for mistakes you have made.

The four Fs for freelancers

So that's my clients kitted out with the four Fs – now it's the freelancers' turn.

Fun

How do you make working with your agency fun for those who work for you? You have to pay them properly, of course, and you need to respect their work, but otherwise you do it in much the same way as you do for the client – by being nice to them. The nicer you are, the more likely they are to go the extra mile for you, to help you out of tight corners and to choose to work for your agency above their other offers.

None of this is business theory, it's the basic algebra of human relations – be good to people and they'll be good to you and your business.

Freedom

Giving freedom to your freelancers is equally straightforward. Essentially, it means leaving them alone to get on with their work. People generally perform best when they are happy and the more you trust them to get on with it the happier they will be. Of course, you need to quality-check their output, especially if they haven't worked for you before, but if you're constantly watching over them, they won't be happy and the quality of their work will suffer.

You should also allow your freelancers the freedom to turn down work without fear that you won't use them again. And you should let them work when and where they like.

Whether they are at their desk or in their favourite crack den, it doesn't matter, as long as they deliver to the agreed standard and deadline.

It's the basic algebra of human relations – be good to people and they'll be good to you and your business.

Flexibility

Primarily, this is all about enabling them to build their working life around their personal priorities – just as you do. Of course, that's what most freelancers do anyway – it's why they're freelance.

You must respect this way of living and working. Allow them to work where and when they like, to pick and choose what work they do and to take time off without fear that they will lose out as a result.

Fairness?

Again, it's easy: pay them the best rates that you can, while leaving yourself a reasonable margin; pay as quickly as you can; don't take sole credit for their work and don't blame them when things go wrong.

For more on how to deal with freelancers, see Leg 3: Collaborators.

Shout the F-words from the rooftops

Research has time and again proved that companies with a strong, positive culture do better than those that don't. As I said earlier, the reasons are simple – clients and employees alike want to work with them.

However, to exploit the benefits of your culture, you need to shout about it. Mention it to all our clients and mention it on your company website. Be bold, be direct and, above all, be truthful.

This is what my agency Write Arm's *Culture and values* page says. As you'll see, it majors on those four Fs and adds a fifth one for good measure – Family.

We like the F-word.

*Correction, we like F-words. Four of them are at the heart of our culture: **Family, Freedom, Flexibility and Fairness.***

*We unashamedly put **Family** first. When John Ashton founded Write Arm his aim was to build a working life around his family. He kept quiet about it until he noticed that most of our writers and clients wanted the same for themselves. So, we now encourage everyone who works for us to follow John's examples. Their work doesn't suffer as a result, it gets better.*

Freedom and Flexibility *go together. Our clients are free to use our services when they want and how they want. We don't tie them in to contracts and we don't insist on retainers. We're entirely flexible – we provide the writers they need, when they need them and we adapt to any system of working that they wish (any reasonable one at least).*

Our writers enjoy freedom and flexibility too. They can work how and when they like – whether from their desk, a café or a mountain top. We try to avoid micromanaging them because we know that people do their best work when free from critical scrutiny.

*And **Fairness**? Simple: we treat our clients and writers fairly. We don't view clients solely as revenue streams. We want to contribute to their* *success. We are honest, we charge reasonably, not excessively, and we're loyal to our writers and pay them decent rates. We don't chase work at all costs and would rather turn down jobs than make a promise that we can't keep.*

Fairness depends on giving value. We're not the most expensive writing service, but we're also not the cheapest. We value what our writers do and pay them accordingly. Our value to clients is based, not only on the quality of our work, but also on the quality of our service.

*Which brings us on to another important word. Happily, it begins with F too. It's **Fun**. We don't wear red noses, we don't have a pool table or a beer fridge and we don't do away days. We're nevertheless on a mission to spread happiness, not to the whole planet, obviously, but at least to our clients and writers.*

We believe that what we do should be enjoyable for all concerned. We work with a smile on our faces and we ask all our writers to do the same, even when they're inwardly grimacing. Remembering that the customer is always right, even when they're wrong, helps everyone to stay happy (and sane).

*There's a final important word that's very dear to us and, believe it or not, it doesn't begin with an F. It's **Giving**. More than most businesses, Write Arm is built upon relationships. Much of our work comes through referrals and we actively seek referrals for our clients and those in our wider network. We gain through giving.*

Are we perfect? Yes, of course we are. OK, we're not, we're human. Occasionally things go wrong. When they do, we don't look for someone to blame, we try to understand and, most importantly, we focus on solutions. It sounds like vacuous business-speak, but it really matters. Dwelling on problems and on who's to blame causes stress and delays solutions. Finding fixes is good for the soul and even better for business.

MY BIGGEST MISTAKE: LEG 1

I ADMIT IT. WHEN I SET UP WRITE ARM, I DIDN'T ASK WHY? OR, AT LEAST I DIDN'T ANSWER THE QUESTION THE RIGHT WAY.

AT THE TIME, THE WHY SEEMED OBVIOUS: I NEEDED TO FEED MY FAMILY AND HAVE FLEXIBILITY. I DIDN'T GO BEYOND THIS TO ASK IF IT WOULD MAKE ME CONTENT.

IT WAS ONLY AS THE COMPANY GREW THAT I BEGAN TO LOVE WHAT I DID. I WAS LUCKY. MANY PEOPLE SET UP A BUSINESS FOR THE SAME REASON THAT I DID AND END UP HATING IT.

LEG TWO

CLIENTS

3 | Honing your offer

Clients: can't live without them, can't live without them

The plane hit the runway with a terrible bump. Our one-year-old son laughed, but all around us passengers looked panicked. I was panicking too. Except it wasn't the bump that worried me. What worried me was the uncontrollable twitch in my eyelid.

It was autumn 2012. We were visiting my brother-in-law in northern Spain. I should have been looking forward to a lovely family holiday, but I was wracked with fear. It wasn't the landing but my company's take-off that was worrying me. Write Arm had been going for six months and my number of clients was a big fat zero. I was watching our savings shrink and my anxieties rise. All kinds of dark thoughts crossed my mind: Would we have to sell the house?

Would I have to take a job stacking shelves? Would I have to send our son out to sweep chimneys?

Now a new fear came to the forefront: was stress taking a major toll on my health? The twitching eyelid seemed to scream the answer – yes!

Fast-forward six years and Write Arm is on course to turn over half a million pounds, I'm as financially secure as I have ever been and, all in all, life is looking rather rosy. The twitch in my eyelid is a distant memory.

A few weeks after I returned from our holiday, I started to get clients. First one, then a steady stream and eventually lots of them. As I write, Write Arm has around 200 clients. Some of them one-off, some are occasional and, most importantly, many of them high-value, long-term ones.

It's blindingly obvious, but I'll say it anyway: if you want to grow your agency, you need more clients. Less obviously, they need to be the right sort of clients – ones who'll be with you for the long term, who appreciate what you do and who have money to spend.

In this leg we'll look at how to identify the best clients, how to get them and how to keep them. But, before we can do that, you need to answer some fundamental questions about your business.

More big questions

So, you're starting your KitchenTable agency? Great choice: bet you can't wait to hit those clients and start enjoying fun, flexible work and a great income? After all, you know what services you'll be offering and you've decided on the values and culture that are at your agency's foundation.

Whoa there, not so fast. Before you start approaching

potential clients, you have to answer three very important questions:

1. What is my mission?
2. What am I selling?
3. Why would clients want to hire my agency?

Let's deal with each of these in turn.

1. What's my mission?

For the past couple of decades mission statements have been a must-have for all organisations. You'll see them on printed on letterheads, in email footers, on banners and, sometimes, literally carved in stone. They range from elegant to clumsy and from profound to profoundly vacuous ('Striving for excellence' anyone?).

When done well, mission statements can help drive organisations forward and make them stand out from the competition. When done badly, they make the organisation a laughing stock and demoralise staff.

A mission isn't essential for your business, but, if you want it to succeed, it sure as hell helps to have one. That's because it's a reference point for everything you do, which can keep you on the straight and narrow as you realise your ambitions.

Your mission must be founded in your culture's underlying values, but it must also have a business goal at its heart. I aimed high with mine – impossibly high: my mission was to make Write Arm the writing resource of choice for all UK marketers.

Of course, not all UK marketers will ever have heard of Write Arm, unless I go on a killing spree, or marry a minor royal. And, even if all of them knew of the company, not all of them would be inclined to hire us. However, thinking big in this way kept me focused on growth and helped hone my decision making.

A mission isn't essential for your business, but, if you want it to succeed, it sure as hell helps to have one.

2.What am I selling?

Now, here's the rub. Unless you have something credible to sell there is no point in having a mission. If your mission was to have a Michelin-starred restaurant and you only serve Pot Noodles, you would look ridiculous. Likewise, if I tried to fulfil Write Arm's mission by outsourcing all of the writing to my seven-year-old son and his classmates.

It took me a while to hone Write Arm's offer, but it was worth every second. It proved to be loved by those who matter: my clients. Distilled to a single line the offer was:

A flexible writing resource for marketers.

Expanded to an elevator pitch it was:

Marketing agencies and in-house marketing teams often struggle to find the writers they need, when they need them. We rid them of that hassle. Our promise is that we shall always find them writers to match their specific needs and budgets. We do this by employing only trusted freelancers, rather than staff writers who might not always fit the bill.

We are, in effect, a one-stop shop that's open 24/7 and we can scale up or down depending on the size of the project. If a client requires a particular expertise that is not covered by our existing pool, we will go and find the right writer for them.

Far be it from me to tell you what your core offer should be. But I'm going to anyway. At least I'm going to tell you the single line version. It should be:

A flexible [insert your area of expertise, e.g. design, web build, digital marketing] *resource for* [insert your target markets, e.g. universities, restaurants, sports clubs].

What I'm about to say is so important that I'm going to write it in capitals: I BELIEVE THAT THE RAISON D'ETRE OF MOST KITCHENTABLE AGENCIES IS TO BE A FLEXIBLE RESOURCE – ONE THAT PROVIDES CLIENTS WITH THE RIGHT FREELANCERS FOR THEIR NEEDS, RATHER THAN OFFERING THEM THE MEMBER OF STAFF WHO HAPPENS TO BE AVAILABLE.

As we'll see shortly, this is so important because it's intimately bound up with the third question: *Why would clients want to hire my agency?* But let's first finish off dealing with the question of what you're selling.

Keep it niche

If you're starting a KitchenTable agency, it's not enough to just duplicate the services that you personally offered as a freelancer or staffer. That's a safe starting place, but it limits your potential. With Write Arm I took on writers who could do a lot more than I could and that greatly widened my potential client base.

Be careful, though. The temptation is to keep bolting on new services, in the belief that you're surely likely to attract more clients. But this just isn't the case. I strongly advise you to restrict your services to a narrow suite. There are two main reasons for this.

The first is that you need to stay within your depth. Let's say you're a branding specialist who has little or no idea about web coding. If you're pitching branding projects to clients then you'll naturally come over as knowledgeable and authoritative. But, if you're pitching web build projects, the chances are that you'll come unstuck. So, stick to what you know.

The second reason is that the more niche you are the more likely it is that your agency will become a sought-after specialist in its field. If you only offer branding, then you will become known as a branding agency, but if you branch out in to web design and build, and other creative services, then you're much less likely to be known as a specialist in branding or any other of the disciplines that you cover.

For the same reason, you should also consider limiting your target market. It's counter intuitive, but the narrower your market the better your chance of success. So, if you have a branding agency, think of the sectors in which you've had the greatest success. If, say, it's food, then you should consider positioning yourself as a specialist food branding agency. That way you'll have a much higher profile in the field – and far fewer competitors – than if you were a general branding agency.

The thing to remember about all this is that nothing need be cast in stone. By applying the wisdom that you gain from experience, you can evolve your service offer as you go.

Ditch the one-man band

Finally, always remember, you're offering the services as an agency. To do that you cannot just be a freelancer who farms out work to friends when you're too busy to do it yourself. There are any number of 'agencies' who do that and most will flatter to deceive. You can generally spot them because the *About us* section of their website only mentions one person. Often it contains a phrase like, 'We work with a network of trusted professionals'. If that's your approach, you will struggle to get larger clients, because they will see that you're a one-man band and a would-be jack of all trades.

3. Why would clients want to hire my agency?

By now you should have worked out your mission and your client offering, both founded around your culture and values. These will be a huge part of your draw to clients. To really fly you still need more: you need to sharply define your offering so that you stand out from the competition like a satanist in a seminary.*

Differentiation, of course, has a lot to do with the services that you offer – the things you nailed when answering '*What am I selling?*' For example, if you offer videos for the luxury goods market, then you have a key differentiator that makes you stand out from most other video production agencies.

However, your services are only part of the story. There are two much more important factors, which you must get right if your agency is going to fly: your selling points and your brand.

---

*Okay, like a sunflower in a field of daisies.

Your selling points

Your selling points are not the services that you sell. Your selling points are the reasons for buying your services. Another way to look at this is that your services are what you are selling and your selling points are what you're *really* selling.

Selling points are often called unique selling points – USPs – but, let's drop the pretence, your agency is not Rolls Royce or Rolex – what it offers is very unlikely to be unique. That said, if they are well-defined and well-articulated, then you can differentiate yourself from most of your competition.

For any business there is a range of factors that might attract clients. If you list those that might attract clients to a creative agency, your list will look something like this:

1. Pricing
2. Quality of work
3. Meeting deadlines
4. The range of services offered
5. The range of industry niches covered
6. Convenience
7. A willingness to be a white label resource
8. Company culture
9. Funky offices
10. The willingness of account managers to regularly get them horribly drunk.

Successful companies score highly on all those factors, right? Wrong. In fact, they concentrate on just some of them and don't compete on the others. Some they may not even offer.

With my agency, Write Arm, we of course put freedom,

flexibility, fairness and fun to the fore. At the same time, we offer a highly responsive, personal service that sees all client enquiries answered promptly by someone who is in tune with their needs and who can ensure that deadlines are met.

Part of our promise is that we provide writers to match any reasonable brief and budget – this often means going out and finding people, if the right ones are not available within our existing talent pool. For hard-pressed marketing teams and agencies, that's a really attractive proposition, because, as well as saving them time and hassle, it means they get better results than they might if they were relying on unvetted freelance suppliers.

When I began the agency, I had no idea just what a potent selling point this was, but, after numerous conversations with marketing managers, account handlers and client services directors, it became clear that handling a bank of freelancers was a major drain on their time and an aggravation that they could do without. They loved the idea of working with someone who could remove that burden by being the single point of contact for sourcing writers.

Taken together, all of this covers items three, five, six, seven and eight (meeting deadlines, range of industry niches, convenience, willingness to be a white label resource and company culture).

We also score well on item two: quality. There are plenty of other content and copywriting providers out there, but few are able to custom match writers to client projects in the way that we are. This is because they tend to either have all their writers on staff, which means they can only offer a relatively narrow range of writing, or they offer a web portal-based service, such as PeoplePerHour or Upwork, which usually put the onus on clients to find the right people.

As for item one, pricing, Write Arm is competitive, but not at the expense of quality. Numerous clients have told us that they came to us after having bad experiences with much cheaper suppliers. To them we still represent good value, because we deliver to the standard that they require and so save them hassle. Others come to us because we cost significantly less than many bricks and mortar agencies.

We also score well on pricing because we don't insist on retainers. Not that all KitchenTable agencies should do the same, but for many of your potential clients, freedom from retainers will be a major turn on.

You might think that item four, the range of services offered, would be a great selling point, but not for me. I could have offered all kinds of spin-off services, such as content marketing and design for print, but I opted not to and it stood me in good stead, because clients knew us for one thing and one thing only, and, as a consequence, they remembered us.

That only leaves the last two items (funky offices and a willingness to get clients horribly drunk). On these two, since we are a virtual agency, we can't compete, which makes our life simpler and saves a fortune in rent, business rates and Nurofen.

Defining your brand (branding specialists can skip this section)

Having well-defined selling points is central to successfully differentiating your company from the opposition, but it's not the only factor that matters. To stand out you also have to project a personality and at the heart of that is your brand. A brand is like art – most people know it when they see it, but they also struggle to define it.

Rather than wage my own struggle, I took the easy way out and turned to Google. Here are three definitions that came up at the top of the results when I typed in 'What is a brand?'

Unique design, sign, symbol, words, or a combination of these, employed in creating an image that identifies a product and differentiates it from its competitors.
BusinessDictionary.com

The personality that identifies a product, service or company (name, term, sign, symbol, or design, or combination of them) and how it relates to key constituencies: customers, staff, partners, investors, etc.
Wikipedia

Your brand is your promise to your customer. It tells them what they can expect from your products and services, and it differentiates your offering from that of your competitors. Your brand is derived from who you are, who you want to be and who people perceive you to be.
Entrepreneur.com

Of these definitions I like the last one best. The first is, of course, right to focus on image and the tangible things, like design, symbols and words, that bring brands to life. And the second is spot on with the personality analogy. The last one edges it though because it nails the fact that brand is all about who you are and want to be. As long as you genuinely know who you are and what you want to be, then you have nailed it too.

Your brand is derived from who you are, who you want to be and who people perceive you to be.

Spelling out your culture

Who you are is, of course, inextricably bound up with your company culture and the values that drive it. So, a crucial element of building your brand is to spell out your culture in the clearest terms – on your website, in your company literature, social media profiles, videos and spray painted across your office.

Sounding different (copywriters can skip this section)

Having something to say is one thing, but knowing how to say it is – surprise, surprise – quite another. It can be hard. Sometimes very hard. The key is to find your authentic voice, then to craft that voice in a way that stands out from the crowd.

Corporations often spend vast sums – much of it with creative agencies – trying to find their tone of voice. You don't need to. Instead just follow our three simple rules, opposite.

Creating your look

When I first set up Write Arm, I knew how I wanted the company to sound – I'm a writer after all – but had no clue about how I wanted to look. I needed to get a website live as soon as possible and, in my rush, didn't devote much time to thinking about how it should look. I just wanted something simple and functional. I briefed an excellent designer as best I could and he came up with just what I wanted.

The trouble was, it looked like any number of other websites. Through no fault of the designer's, it just looked bland. It could

HOW TO DEVELOP YOUR VOICE

SPEAK AS YOU WISH TO BE SPOKEN TO

LOOK AT A FEW CLIENTS' AND COMPETITORS' WEBSITES AND FIND THOSE THAT YOU FIND MOST ENGAGING. READ THESE OVER A FEW TIMES. IT'S A POWERFUL EXERCISE THAT CAN WORK WONDERS IN HELPING YOU DEVELOP YOUR OWN STYLE.

CUT THE CRAP

TO STAND OUT YOU NEED TO BE SPARING WITH WORDS. DON'T USE FIVE WHERE ONE WILL DO AND DON'T USE ANY WHERE NONE WILL DO. ALWAYS BE DIRECT. IF EVER YOU ARE STRUGGLING, BEAR IN MIND THE FOLLOWING LITTLE EXERCISE. WHICH OF THESE TWO PHRASES WORKS BEST?

WE WOULD LIKE TO WISH YOU EVERY HAPPINESS ON THIS DAY, WHICH IS THE ANNIVERSARY OF YOUR BIRTH

OR

HAPPY BIRTHDAY TO YOU

NO CONTEST EH? YET TOO MANY PEOPLE WRITE THEIR WEBSITES IN THE FORMER STYLE IN THE BELIEF THAT FORMALITY AND WORDINESS ATTRACT CUSTOMERS. THEY DON'T. AT LEAST THEY DON'T IN THE CREATIVE INDUSTRIES.

IF IN DOUBT, HIRE A COPYWRITER

THIS IS NOT ME TOUTING FOR WORK FOR WRITE ARM, IT'S JUST SENSIBLE ADVICE IF YOU'RE STRUGGLING. GOOD COPYWRITERS ARE NOT DIFFICULT TO FIND AND, IF YOU HAVE A REAL PROBLEM WITH WORDS, THEY CAN SPARE YOU A LOT OF AGONY.

have been built for a law firm or a GP practice. There was no visual statement about what the company did and how it was different, because I had failed to give the matter any thought.

When, four years later, I got a new site I took time to think about what I really wanted and needed. As I had a writing agency, I decided that the look should be heavily typographical. I also wanted it to be bold, in order to complement the company's direct, humorous tone of voice and to stand out from other writing agencies. I wanted a simple main menu consisting of five words: Who (covering our writers and clients), What (covering the services offered and a portfolio), Why (covering the main selling points and testimonials), Where (contact details) and Whatever (blog).

Armed with that wish list I sat down with a different designer, the brilliant Joel at the Brighton-based digital agency Madison Solutions. A couple of days later he sent me a list of sites which he thought had a similar feel to what I wanted. We then sat down again and I told him which ones I liked and whether it was their layout, colour palette or use of text that attracted me.

Joel then went away and worked on some initial designs. He suggested a vertically split screen that mimicked the open pages of a book. The left side was always black and contained the five-word main menu, which ran down the side using an outsized sans serif font. The text only appeared on right side against the background of a bold contrasting colour, which switched with each of the five main menu items. It was complemented by a great new logo.

I was delighted. It was love at first sight. It only took a little tweaking to get the look spot on. I have rarely seen a site that looks as distinctive as Write Arm's. I am sure that not everyone likes it, but the majority who see it do, and many of them *really* like it. More importantly, they remember it. It says that Write Arm is different and interesting and, if you think a

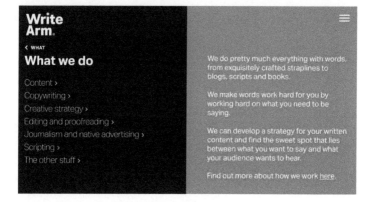

Screen grabs of Write Arm's website

company is different and interesting, you are likely to give them a call.

So, now you have answered those three important questions:

1. *What is my mission?*
2. *What am I selling?*
3. *Why would clients want to hire my agency?*

That's enough about you. Now it's time to talk about clients.

Identifying client types: The ones you need to attract... and the ones you don't

Clients come in all shapes and sizes, but broadly speaking your KitchenTable agency is likely to attract three main types.

- The first is owner-managed businesses that are too small to have a marketing team
- The second is larger businesses that have a marketing team
- And the third is other agencies.

Let's look at them in turn.

Owner-managed businesses

When you start your agency it's quite likely that the first clients to come through the door will be small business owner-managers. If you've been a freelancer you've probably already have such clients.

At one level owner-managers are a natural fit for your business. They run their own enterprise, they really care about what they do and they pay attention to detail. They are generally ambitious too. What's not to like?

Actually, quite a lot. Don't get me wrong, owner-managers can be great – indeed they have been some of my best clients. However, most of the troublesome jobs we have ever done have come from these client types. I still take on owner-manager clients, but only once I have assured myself that they really know what they want and that they have ambitions to grow into a good long-term client. The others I politely decline and point them in the direction of freelancers whom I trust to do a good job for them.

Larger clients

To qualify for this category the client must have a marketing department. That department might consist of only one person or it might have a whole team; it doesn't really matter. What counts is that they have a marketing budget and if they have a marketing budget then, chances are, they will need to outsource at least some of their creative output. And who better to outsource to than your KitchenTable agency?

The great thing about working with marketers – and this

FOUR REASONS TO BE WARY OF OWNER-MANAGED BUSINESSES

1. THEY ARE NOT MARKETERS OR CREATIVES

PLUMBERS PLUMB, ACCOUNTANTS KNOW ABOUT NUMBERS, IT COMPANIES KNOW ABOUT IT. FAIR ENOUGH. THE PROBLEM CAN BE THAT OFTEN THEY OFTEN DON'T KNOW MUCH ABOUT MARKETING OR WHAT GOOD CREATIVE OUTPUT LOOKS LIKE. MOREOVER, WHILE THEY OFTEN DON'T REALLY KNOW WHAT THEY WANT, THEY GENERALLY KNOW WHAT THEY DON'T WANT. AND, TOO OFTEN WHAT THEY DON'T WANT IS WHAT YOU DELIVER. I DON'T WISH TO EXAGGERATE THIS PROBLEM — IN THE GREAT MAJORITY OF CASES THESE CLIENTS HAVE BEEN HAPPY WITH OUR WORK — BUT THEY ARE NEVERTHELESS DISPROPORTIONATELY LIKELY TO TURN UP THEIR NOSES AT OUR WORK.

2. THEY TEND TO BE VERY COST CONSCIOUS

WHEN YOU RUN YOUR OWN BUSINESS, EVERY PENNY COUNTS. SO, EVERY ITEM OF EXPENDITURE IS SCRUTINISED. AS A RESULT, BUDGETS TEND TO BE TIGHT AND YOU'LL OFTEN BE SCREWED DOWN ON COSTS. THEY MIGHT EVEN OFFER TO PAY YOU IN TOILET ROLLS OR CABBAGES.

3. MISSION CREEP

OWNER MANAGERS' DETERMINATION TO LOCK DOWN BUDGETS IS OFTEN ACCOMPANIED BY A TENDENCY TO STEALTHILY EXPAND JOB SPECS. I HAVE LOST COUNT OF THE NUMBER OF TIMES THAT AN OWNER MANAGER HAS EXPECTED US TO DO WORK THAT WAS NOT INCLUDED IN THE ORIGINAL BRIEF.

ON POINTING THIS OUT, I'VE OFTEN HAD A RESPONSE ALONG THE LINES OF: 'MONEY IS TIGHT AT THE MOMENT, BUT WE ARE AN EXPANDING BUSINESS AND WANT TO WORK WITH YOU LONG TERM.' SOMETIMES THIS 'JAM TOMORROW' PROMISE WORKS OUT, BUT OFTEN IT DOESN'T.

---

4. PROJECTS TEND TO BE AD HOC AND ONE-OFF

SMALL ONE-OFF PROJECTS ARE OK – AND, WHEN YOU START YOUR AGENCY THEY MAY WELL BE ITS LIFEBLOOD – BUT WHAT YOU REALLY NEED IS ON-GOING WORK THAT WILL PROVIDE YOU WITH A STEADY INCOME. IN MY EXPERIENCE, OWNER-MANAGED BUSINESSES RARELY PROVIDE THESE UNTIL THEY HAVE GROWN TO A GOOD SIZE. THAT MIGHT TAKE YEARS AND YOU PROBABLY CAN'T AFFORD TO HANG AROUND.

I STILL TAKE ON OWNER-MANAGER CLIENTS, BUT ONLY ONCE I HAVE ASSURED MYSELF THAT THEY REALLY KNOW WHAT THEY WANT AND THAT THEY HAVE AMBITIONS TO GROW INTO A GOOD LONG-TERM CLIENT. THE OTHERS I POLITELY DECLINE AND POINT THEM IN THE DIRECTION OF FREELANCERS WHOM I TRUST TO DO A GOOD JOB FOR THEM.

---

goes for agencies too – is that they generally know the value of what agencies like yours do. Better still, they know what they want and they know quality when they see it.

This all means that, when compared to small owner-managed businesses, they are less likely to quibble over budgets, less likely to reject your work and more likely provide you with a regular income.

In many ways then they are the holy grail. The only drawback in my experience, especially with very large companies, is that they can be bureaucratic and hierarchical. This sometimes means that they are slow to greenlight projects and occasionally results in the marketing team's plans to use your agency being thwarted. Don't let any of this put you off though – if you really want your agency to thrive, larger clients are essential.

Creative agencies

You have set up your own agency, so why would you want to work for another agency? The actual question should be why would you not want to? Unlike many owner-managed businesses, agencies speak the language of marketing and creativity. In other words, they tend to get what you do better than anyone else.

Creative agencies come in all shapes and sizes. There are traditional advertising agencies, design and branding based ones, web development agencies, digital marketing agencies, some of which focus on SEO; others on social media and some on PPC-driven lead generation. There are audio visual production agencies encompassing everything from traditional video production companies to VR and AR specialists. There are also infinite combinations of the above.

Within them you'll find flamboyant creatives, genius techies, cerebral journalists, data crunchers and marketing wizards. What you won't find, if you keep your mind open, is anyone dull. That alone is good enough reason to work with agencies. But there is a much more significant reason. Many agencies don't do everything in-house and are only too happy to farm out work to reliable partner agencies. I've been observing the agency scene for some years now and during that time the outsourcing of creative production has become the new norm, even for some of the industry's largest players. Older agencies have reduced the size of their creative teams in order to cut overheads, while many younger, more agile ones have business models that are explicitly based on outsourcing.

So, the agency market has never been so fertile – get out there and sow your seed.

5 | Getting clients - commonly known as marketing

If, as I did, you start your agency with no clients, then getting your first one can feel like trying to move a giant boulder. It's hard because you're in a classic Catch 22: clients are reluctant to hire an agency with no track record and without clients you can't get a track record.

Eventually though the boulder will move. Someone will come along who trusts you and, once they have, you'll have the momentum, more work is likely to flow your way and you can breathe easily.

How then can you best get clients? Or, to put it another way, what should your marketing strategy be? The answer, of course, is largely dependent upon the size of your marketing budget. Let's assume it's the same as mine was when I started Write Arm – close to zero.

Marketing with (almost) no budget

There is one word that should define your approach to marketing, especially if you have little or nothing to spend. Is it Sell, Grab, Persuade, Pitch, Plead, Cry? No. The word is Give. Yes, you read that correctly, Give.

Giving should be at the core of your marketing strategy. People really appreciate givers and tend to both like and remember them. This means that they are likely to put work your way, or refer you to other potential clients.

Giving should be at the core of your marketing strategy. People really appreciate givers and tend to both like and remember them.

But what does giving look like in this context? Signing over your house or your life savings? Letting them take your children – or, worse, your car? Fortunately not. It can mean all or any of the following:

• Referring them to clients who want services that your agency can't offer
• Introducing them to other agencies if you think there might be useful synergies between them
• Introducing them to potential employees
• Pointing them to useful suppliers, tools and resources
• Buying them coffee
• Giving them your hamster.

There are two great things about a giving-led strategy aside from the fact that it delivers results. The first is simply that it feels good. Who doesn't like to give? It bestows you that lovely warm feeling, like bathing in chocolate. The second is that it takes the strain out of marketing. It means you don't have to sell, persuade, make cold calls or sleep with anyone you would rather not.

Don't give with the expectation that your beneficiaries should reciprocate – that's deal making, rather than real giving. Not that you should be averse to making deals, of course, but it shouldn't be your primary strategy.

Finding prospects

The digital explosion of the last couple of decades has spawned plenty of smart ways to grab the attention of potential clients – a.k.a. prospects. But let's assume that you don't have the budget for the more expensive ones, like paid advertising, and lack the time for the slower burning, time-consuming ones, like social media marketing. Happily, you still have plenty of options. Let's look at the main ones.

Cold contact

This usually means contacting a prospect out of the blue. Unless you're a born salesperson, then my advice is don't try calling. It's a fast route to disillusionment. It's generally a hard slog, not least because the reaction tends to range from mild irritation to murderous rage. After all, if you hate receiving cold sales calls – and who doesn't – why wouldn't your prospects?

Emailing is a much better bet than phoning, but only if you can distinguish your emails from the scores of spam emails that prospects receive from digital agencies every week. It's essential that you don't use email marketing lists. Instead, identify your prospects by googling or trawling LinkedIn, then find their email addresses, which usually takes a bit more googling and sometimes some rational deduction.

There is another golden rule of emailing. Always follow up. Don't make a nuisance of yourself, but be gently persistent. If you get no response. Always try at least two polite follow ups. Cold emailing should get you better results than cold calling, but, done well, they take time – time that might be better spent on other activities.

Client referrals

Referrals by your clients are wonderful things – after all, who better to introduce you to prospects than a happy customer? Hopefully, when your agency is well established, they'll come flooding in. The catch is, of course, that until you have clients there's no one to give you client referrals.

Once you have some satisfied clients, you shouldn't be shy about politely asking them for referrals. Be sure to make a reciprocal offer though – you should always aim to give at least as much as you receive, if at all possible.

Networking

Here's a bold statement: Networking is the quickest and most cost-effective way of getting clients. Correction: *When done right*, networking is the quickest and most cost-effective way of getting clients. Take my word for it – if you want to grow your business and have no decent marketing budget,

HOW TO GET CLIENT REFERRALS

IT'S A COMMON SCENARIO. YOU'VE DONE A GREAT JOB FOR A CLIENT AND THEY'RE ONLY TOO HAPPY TO GIVE YOU REFERRALS. THE TROUBLE IS, THEY ARE TOO BUSY TO DO IT. THE ONLY WAY TO MAKE IT HAPPEN IS TO TAKE THE LEAD.

FIRST, YOU HAVE TO FIND THE PROSPECTS THAT YOU'D LIKE TO BE INTRODUCED TO. THE EASIEST WAY TO DO THIS IS TO GO THROUGH YOUR CLIENT'S LINKEDIN CONNECTIONS AND MAKE A LIST OF YOUR TOP TARGETS. THEN YOU HAVE TO COMPOSE EMAILS TO ALL OF THEM THAT YOUR CLIENT CAN SIMPLY CUT AND PASTE AND SEND. THEY WILL THANK YOU FOR SAVING THEM SO MUCH TIME.

get out there and network.

Until a few years ago I would rather have spent a couple of weeks being roasted alive by Beelzebub than spend a couple of hours in a roomful of businessfolk. These days I love it, in fact it's one of my favourite pastimes. Here's how my attitude changed and, if you hate networking as much as I did, you can change yours.

Take my word for it – if you want to grow your business and have no decent marketing budget, get out there and network.

There are two essentials, neither of them are rocket science so anyone can master them. The first is to get over your fears. Very few people feel no awkwardness at networking events and everyone was a first-timer once. If you're anxious about entering a room full of strangers, then ask yourself the obvious question: what's the worst that can happen? The answer is that you could get horribly drunk, vomit on one of your prize prospects, start a fight and be arrested. It could happen, but it probably won't, especially if you stick to mineral water.

The worst that is likely to happen is that you have a few lame conversations with people who are uninterested in your business and just want to give you the hard sell. It happened to me a few times, until I learnt which events were worth attending and which were a waste of time.

The second essential can be summed up in two words: Don't Sell. It's a cliché, but, with the exception of shopaholics, no one likes being sold to, especially serial networkers.

Networking isn't just about attending networking events, it's about growing a network. Events are a great way to do it, but they are not the only way. Think of how you grew your social network. Events, like parties and dinners doubtless played a role, but one-to-one time with new acquaintances was likely equally important. Like at school, university or your sports club, you meet someone, have a brief conversation, then arrange to meet them at greater length over a coffee, a beer or a few lines of crystal meth.

And this is how it should be with your network. It's great to meet someone at an event, but chances are that, unless you follow up with a one-to-one, you are not going to develop the mutual bond that will bring good things to you both.

Don't only look to meet prospective clients. You should meet anyone you can, especially in the early days of your agency when you're still finding your feet. That includes business owners who are never likely to be clients, it includes suppliers and it even includes competitors.

THE £50K CUP OF COFFEE

A FEW YEARS AGO, I WENT FOR A COFFEE WITH THE OWNER OF A LARGE WEB DEVELOPMENT AGENCY. HE DIDN'T NEED A COPYWRITER AND WAS NEVER LIKELY TO, SO I DIDN'T VIEW HIM AS A POTENTIAL CLIENT. I JUST FANCIED A CHAT AND SO DID HE. WE GOT ON WELL AND AT THE END OF THE MEETING HE OFFERED TO INTRODUCE ME TO A COUPLE OF DIGITAL MARKETING AGENCIES OWNERS WHOM HE KNEW.

HE WAS AS GOOD AS HIS WORD. ONE OF THE OWNERS ASKED FOR A MEETING AND WITHIN WEEKS HAD BECOME A SIGNIFICANT CLIENT. TO DATE WE HAVE INVOICED THAT AGENCY FOR OVER £50,000 OF WORK.

SO, KEEP YOUR CAPPUCCINOS AT THE READY – YOU NEVER KNOW WHEN THEY'LL COME IN HANDY.

6 | Keeping clients

Getting clients can be hard, sometimes very hard. But it's not the end of the story: to be truly successful your business depends on keeping them. There is no fool-proof formula for keeping clients, but fortunately if you follow the advice in the earlier chapters you shouldn't have too much difficulty in retaining most of them. So, we can keep this chapter nice and short.

Even if your output is always stellar, you remain at the mercy of a whole lorry load of factors over which you have no control. Among them are clients' changing budgetary priorities, personnel changes, the world economy, the alignment of the planets and the secret manoeuvrings of the Illuminati. There are, however, simple steps you can take to mitigate some of the risks.

Work on relationships

Relationships are at the core of life and therefore they're at the core of business. It's likely that some of your clients will become friends, maybe even close friends. Who knows, you might even end up in bed with them.* Most won't be friends though. But that misses the point. Friendship is the icing on the cake. What you really need is clients' loyalty.

To get loyalty you must, first and foremost, give it. The first essential of building loyalty is pretty basic – you must be friendly. You don't have to be friends to be friendly. I'm friendly with the staff of my local off licence, but I've never invited them home to share a bottle of White Lightning.

Being friendly doesn't only mean being cheery. It means being sympathetic when people are ill or in difficulty, it means enquiring about their weekend and their family, it means sending them a handwritten Christmas card and it means holding your tongue when you're stressed or they have pissed you off. It means all these things and a thousand more.

I'm lucky, as being friendly comes naturally. If it doesn't come naturally to you, then work on it – it's worth it.

How's my driving?

If you lose a client, you might have seen it coming a mile off. But, then again, you might not. Most agency owners whom I know have told me that when they lose a client it usually comes as a bolt from the blue but, in hindsight, it happened because they were unaware that a client was unhappy.

---

* Disclaimer: I never have – and never would – go further than a peck on the cheek and a hug.

You can mitigate this risk by regularly seeking feedback on your agency's performance. As well as helping you up your game, it reminds your clients that you care. You don't need to do it after every job, but you should aim do it after a major piece of work and do it as a matter of course every few months. Don't lumber them with a questionnaire – a simple email will do it.

To get loyalty you must, first and foremost, give it.

A SIMPLE FEEDBACK EMAIL

HI SARAH,

JUST WANTED TO CHECK THAT EVERYONE AT YOUR END HAS BEEN HAPPY WITH OUR RECENT WORK. IT'S ALWAYS GOOD TO HAVE A BIT OF FEEDBACK – EVEN NEGATIVE – AS IT HELPS US SHARPEN OUR GAME. DO LET ME KNOW IF THERE'S ANYTHING YOU THINK WE CAN IMPROVE.

BEST

JOHN.

Don't be a stranger

If you routinely deal with a number of people within the same organisation, then it's usually worth having occasional meetings, especially if you have only dealt with some of them by email. It's a great way to get feedback and to strengthen personal bonds.

If you only generally deal with one person, then, of course, it's especially important to retain a strong bond. What then, if they leave the company, or are promoted to a job in which they will no longer be dealing with you? There is always a danger that their replacement will want to replace you with their own favoured supplier.

As soon as you know that your chief contact is about to leave, ask them to introduce you to their replacement. It might be worth teeing up a meeting with the new person.

Finally, don't forget the power of an occasional lunch, or coffee and cake. Getting away from the office is usually a great relaxant, which makes for better conversation and strengthens personal ties.

Prove your value

Business-speak alert. I'm about to write something that you've probably heard a hundred times before. Here goes. Clients don't hire you for the sake of it, they hire you because they need your help to make their business work better. So, cheesy at it may sound, instead of thinking how much work you can get from them, think instead about how you can help them. It's a crucial shift in thinking that should work wonders for you and hopefully for your clients too.

More than anything, it requires deep listening to your clients' aims and pain points. Really make an effort to understand them.

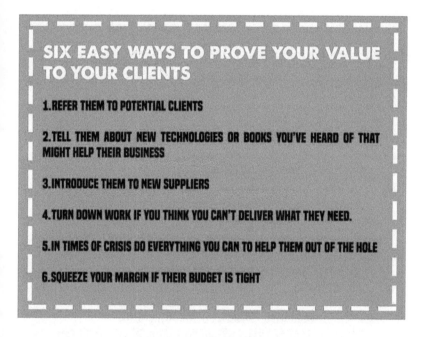

SIX EASY WAYS TO PROVE YOUR VALUE TO YOUR CLIENTS

1. REFER THEM TO POTENTIAL CLIENTS

2. TELL THEM ABOUT NEW TECHNOLOGIES OR BOOKS YOU'VE HEARD OF THAT MIGHT HELP THEIR BUSINESS

3. INTRODUCE THEM TO NEW SUPPLIERS

4. TURN DOWN WORK IF YOU THINK YOU CAN'T DELIVER WHAT THEY NEED.

5. IN TIMES OF CRISIS DO EVERYTHING YOU CAN TO HELP THEM OUT OF THE HOLE

6. SQUEEZE YOUR MARGIN IF THEIR BUDGET IS TIGHT

Things can only get better

Yes, I know it sounds trite, but it happens to be true: you have to keep getting better at everything you do. Happily, unless you are utterly incompetent or are pre-programmed to self-destruct, the longer you run your business, you should get better at everything naturally. Yes, everything – from the big stuff, like quality control, to the little things, like the layout of your quotes and your email signatures.

If you're tempted to think that you don't need to improve, hold this thought: your competitors almost certainly don't think that way and they would be delighted to know that you did.

Unless you are utterly incompetent or are pre-programmed to self-destruct, the longer you run your business, you should get better at everything naturally.

MY BIGGEST MISTAKE: LEG 2

WHEN I SET UP WRITE ARM, I DIDN'T HAVE A WELL-DEFINED PROPOSITION. I OFFERED WRITERS, BUT ALSO THREW IN THE ODD ILLUSTRATOR, A PHOTOGRAPHER AND A DESIGNER. THE PROPOSITION WAS: WE WRITE, BUT WE ALSO DO THESE OTHER THINGS. NO WONDER IT DIDN'T FLY.

I JETTISONED THE NON-WRITING SERVICES, BUT STILL THE PROPOSITION WAS TOO VAGUE. MORE IMPORTANTLY, IT FOCUSED ON WHAT WE DID, RATHER THAN ON WHAT OUR IDEAL CLIENTS MIGHT WANT.

IT WAS ONLY AFTER I'D WORKED OUT WHO THE IDEAL CLIENTS WERE – MARKETING AGENCIES AND IN-HOUSE MARKETING TEAMS – AND REALLY LISTENING TO THEM THAT I LEARNED WHY THEY WANTED TO HIRE US.

IN SHORT, THEY LIKED THE FLEXIBILITY WE OFFERED AND THE FACT THAT WE TOOK THE HASSLE OUT OF FINDING AND HIRING WRITERS. THUS, I FINALLY CAME UP WITH A SIMPLE PROPOSITION FOR THE AGENCY: A FLEXIBLE WRITING RESOURCE FOR MARKETERS.

LEG THREE

COLLABORATORS

CHAPTER

7 | Your greatest asset (and your greatest liability)

You might think that if you're going to run a successful KitchenTable agency then keeping clients happy is far more important than keeping your freelancers happy. Think again.

Though they might not be salaried staff, the people who work for you are your most precious asset and are every bit as important as your clients. You must treat them like treasured staff. This section explains why. It shows you how to attract great freelancers and how to get the very best out of them.

Don't be a bastard

The world is full of good freelance creatives. It's a buyers' market. You're free to pick them and drop them like

Victorian ship owners choosing their crews. When things are so stacked in your favour, you can be as ruthless as you like.

But don't be. Here's why.

Happy workers make for happy clients

Treating people well helps to keep them happy and when people are happy they tend to do their best work. And what does good work mean? Happy clients, of course.

You need a settled team

From the perspective of your clients and prospects, a potential downside of working with your KitchenTable agency is that they won't be able to work with a single individual, or team, and will instead be assigned a random selection of freelancers. You can only allay this fear if you have a settled pool of people who will be happy to work with you and your clients long term. And, guess what, you can only create such a pool if you treat your people well.

News will soon spread

If you don't treat your freelancers well, the grapevine will soon be humming. The news won't only spread to the freelance community, it will also spread to your clients and prospects. You'll soon find that your phone stops ringing and your inbox empties. The only sound to drown out the tumbleweed will be that of your rising panic.

It's bad for the soul

Really, it is.

Treating people well helps to keep them happy and when people are happy they tend to do their best work.

Building loyalty

If your KitchenTable agency is to be successful your freelancers have to consistently be at the top of their game. More importantly, you need to rely on their loyalty.

Imagine that it's six o'clock on Friday and a client tells you they urgently need a piece of work by Monday morning. You're only going to get someone to do the work if you can rely on their loyalty. And you'll only get freelancers' loyalty if they have yours.

That of course means they must stick to the company's rules and values, but it also means that you have obligations to them. They're not on the payroll, so they don't get holiday entitlements, sick pay, use of the company helicopter and all the rest of it. But you still must look after them in every reasonable way.

Reasonable, what's reasonable?

The six pillars of reasonableness (or how to be a good boss)

1. Give your core suppliers all the work that you can

It's inevitable that you will employ some freelancers much more than others. It might be, for example, because you do a lot of work in a particular sector, or because your major clients really like certain people. In time your pool of regulars will expand and, as you become more successful, the expansion will continue.

Any core supplier will have come to rely on you for a sizeable part of their income. If you decided to switch off the tap because you fancied trying out someone else, it could blow a hole in their finances with all the stress and unpleasantness that that brings. So, don't do it. Try to direct a regular flow of work their way.

2. Allow them flexibility

You're probably tired of me banging on about flexibility. Tough. To remind you, flexibility is – or should be – at the core of what you offer, not only to your clients, but also to your suppliers. So, if one of your freelancers turns down work because they have to look after their kids, or have their traction engine restoration club's annual dinner, then don't hold it against them. Allow them the time they need off and find someone else to do the work.

3. Be compassionate

Into every life a little rain must fall. Sometimes the rain turns into what Shakespeare called 'a whole goddam shitstorm'. When that happens to a freelancer it generally means taking time off work and not earning. And that requires you to give them every support that you reasonably can.

A few years ago, a Write Arm freelancer told me that she needed to take some time off. She asked if we could meet for a coffee so she could explain more face-to-face. I agreed, even though I was rushed off my feet at the time.

At the meeting she anxiously confided that she had a chronic health condition, which had reared its head again after a couple of years of dormancy. Aside from her own wellbeing, she was anxious about the difficulty it would cause Write Arm as I had earmarked her for a couple of large projects that had just come in.

I took care to assure her that there would be no problem at my end and, more importantly, that there would be plenty of work for her when she felt well enough to return to work. A few weeks later she was well again and was very soon taking on the usual volume of work from Write Arm.

4. Be forgiving

With the obvious exception of the author of this book, no one is perfect. Everyone screws up sometimes, and even your most trusted people will from time to time make mistakes or produce sub-standard work, as will you. As long as they didn't act dishonestly or maliciously, don't hold it against them, even if their mistake seriously pissed off your client. To err is to be human and, in any case, life is too short to spend accumulating petty resentments.

There are two more practical reasons not to come down on mistakes. Firstly, it's likely to stress the person who messed up, and stressed people don't produce their best work, indeed it leaves them more error prone. Secondly, if you do take a punitive approach, word will soon spread through the freelance community and people won't want to work for you anymore. Freelancers are your life blood – be careful not to cut the artery.

If the client they were working for was unhappy, then it might be wise to offer them another team member to work with. If you do, make sure you give other work to the one who made the mistake. There's no better way of proving your loyalty.

Freelancers are your life blood – be careful not to cut the artery.

5. Carry the can

When things go wrong don't allow your freelancers to take the flak, even if, on the face of it, it's their fault. The buck stops with you, even if you think it doesn't – it really does. 'Why?' I hear you cry, 'If a freelancer screws up, then surely it's their fault.' Erm, yes, but no. If you assigned a freelancer to a project and they didn't do as well as you'd hoped, then that's your responsibility.

Crucially, you must convey this to your client. In my experience, most are forgiving and don't make an issue of it, but occasionally – very occasionally – they will cut up rough. If that happens, you must reiterate the point and, more importantly, do all you can to prevent them from blaming the freelancer.

Any good freelancer will feel wretched about making a mistake and client criticism just compounds their agony. And when they feel that way the quality of their work is likely to suffer. So, it's doubly important to be their human shield. They'll thank you for it (and most clients will respect you for it).

6. Pay properly and pay on time

You can't, of course, pay your freelancers regularly monthly salaries – if you did, they wouldn't be freelance – but, you must look after them financially as far as you're able.

That, of course, means paying them a reasonable rate for the work that they do. As a general rule, you should pay them the best rate that you can while leaving yourself a reasonable margin. If you constantly try to pay them the minimum you can, then they're unlikely to give you their loyalty and best work. Sure, it will provide a temporary boost to your bank balance, but a long-term hit to your business, not to mention your karma.

You should also pay your people as quickly as you can. Ideally that should be as soon as possible after you are paid for the work they did. You need to look after your cashflow – so, as a general rule, you shouldn't pay before you have been paid. However, cashflow allowing, there can be exceptions. For example, if a client is months late in paying, or if a freelancer is obviously in financial difficulty and needs paying urgently to fend off the bailiffs. (It's also wise to pay up if a freelancer turns up at your house with a gun.)

CHAPTER

8 | Finding talent

When you launch your KitchenTable agency, you'll have probably lined up all the talent that you're likely to need. They might be friends, people you have worked with before, friends of friends or people you've met on Tinder. Before long though you're likely to need people with specialist talents that aren't covered within your existing pool. Furthermore, you might need them at very short notice. If you do, then here are the best ways to locate the people you need.

Use online databases

Portals like LinkedIn, Upworks and PeoplePerHour make it easier than ever to find talent. Yet in my experience many clients rarely use them. I have lost count of the number of occasions on which clients have come to me to say they require a particular expert. I have usually found the person they need on LinkedIn within minutes. Why didn't the clients do it themselves? Probably because they don't have time, even for such relatively short tasks.

If you're having trouble finding people through the large portals, remember that there are plenty of useful specialist ones too. On a few occasions, clients have asked me for foreign language copywriters. I quickly learned that, rather than trawling LinkedIn, it was much easier to use Translators Café. It looks awful (at least it does at the time of writing – think late nineties dating site) but it works well and has enabled me to find lots of good people. There are specialist directory sites for many creative professions.

There are also local sites where you can browse the profiles of all kinds of specialists. For example, in Brighton, where I live, Brighton Farm and Wired Sussex are both deep wells of freelance digital talent that include developers, designers, illustrators, writers and probably a few characters from *The Matrix*.

Leverage your network

Not long after I had established Write Arm, a potential client – a digital marketing agency – contacted me with an urgent request for expert B2B technology writers. They had just won a major piece of work with a large IT company and needed specialists to produce articles, case studies and white papers.

If they had asked, 'Do you have any technology writers' I would have had to answer, 'No', because that was the truth. Had I done so, I might have lost the work. Fortunately, they asked, 'Could you supply technology writers?' so I answered honestly, 'Yes'.

After a few moments' panic, I hit the phone. Luckily, it only took one call to get traction. It was to a consumer tech journalist I had met a few weeks earlier. He ruled himself out as a writer, but recommended four others to me, who, as it happened, fitted the bill perfectly. Within a day I was able to tell the client that I had the people they needed. They were very grateful and the assignment turned into two years of regular work.

Don't underestimate the power of your network. It is often the best way of finding reliable freelance creatives.

Warmly welcome cold callers

Within a few weeks of the Write Arm website going live I began to receive enquiries from writers looking for work. I use the term 'writers' loosely. Some clearly couldn't write, in fact, judging by their emails, they might have struggled to tie their shoelaces. One of them described herself as a 'copyrighter' and others would have struggled to pass their English SAT. (Come to think of it, as I never checked their ages, some might have been too young for SATS.)

Among them though were some real gems: like Greg, a stellar comms specialist, Trisha, a demon content strategist and Mat, a superfast copywriter with an encyclopaedic knowledge of SEO. I couldn't give any of them work immediately but within a few months all of them were Write Arm regulars. More importantly they filled holes in the Write Arm's corporate CV or, to put it more bluntly, they made the company look better.

So, if anyone contacts you out of the blue, don't ignore them on the grounds that you have no work for them.

Instead, answer their enquiry politely and ask them to submit their CV and samples of their work. You never know when you might need them.

Don't underestimate the power of your network. It is often the best way of finding reliable freelance creatives.

Keep a database

Well before Write Arm's first anniversary, experience had taught me that I needed to keep a record of all the freelancers who had contacted me. I would strongly advise you to do the same. It doesn't need to be elaborate. All I did was create a spreadsheet that listed writers and their subject specialisms. I then created a virtual folder for each writer where I stored their CVs and samples. Each folder was within a master folder called, with the imagination for which I am renowned, *CVs and samples*.

The same principle would work for other creative and digital professionals, such as designers, photographers and web developers.

When a client asked for a niche specialist I would turn first to the spreadsheet. Often, I needed to look no further, as it threw up the name of at least one specialist. Sometimes though the spreadsheet was not enough and I would have to turn to the folders. As I had way too many writers to remember who did what, I relied upon a simple word search. It was usually enough.

Here's a simple example of the usefulness of the database. Back in 2015 a client asked if I could supply a writer who could write about the importance of nutrition in rugby. A quick look at the spreadsheet provided me with the names of a few writers who were sports specialists and a couple of others who had written about health and nutrition. They were all good writers, but I wasn't convinced that they were the right fit. I did a word search for 'rugby' and 'nutrition' within the *CVs and samples* folder. The search threw up a single document – the CV of a writer called James, whom I had never before used. On reading it I discovered that he had edited the rugby pages of a national newspaper and ghost written a magazine column on fitness and nutrition for an England rugby player. He was, in short, the perfect man for the job. The agency was very pleased and commissioned a series of 70 articles, which James completed with aplomb.

One important thing to note. When writers send you their samples, make sure they are in the form of searchable files like Word or PDF documents, rather than links to web pages.

Vetting

Finding suitable freelancers can take very little time, so why don't clients do more of it themselves? The main reason, which comes up time after time in my conversations with clients, is that finding people is only half the battle – the easy half.

Much more difficult – and time consuming – is ensuring that the freelancers are up to scratch. That involves checking their credentials, asking for samples of their work and speaking to them in order to ensure that they will be a good fit for the project for which they are needed. These are all things that you should be doing. Believe me, clients value it massively and it's essential if you are to maintain your quality standards. It takes time, but it's well worth it.

9 | Some ground rules

You can't have failed to notice that I'm a great believer in leaving freelancers alone to get on with their work. It saves you time, it saves you hassle and it generally leads to better output.

However, to get the best out of people and for the good of your business, you also need to lay out some ground rules that they all understand and abide by.

Remember, you're one of the gang

Your freelancers are not staff, but they are still your employees. If they are to be an asset to your business, then first and foremost they need to know and embrace your culture and values. Of course, they will only do this if you treat them properly – so make sure that you do.

The customer is always right, even when they are wrong

There are plenty of talented creatives out there, all of whom are potential competition, so your KitchenTable agency has to compete on the other available grounds. The most important of these, as I've said before, is the quality of your client interactions. People buy with their hearts rather than their heads. They want to hire people they like and who will make their lives as pleasant as possible. For the most part, this is easy, but isn't so easy when jobs don't go to plan, or when the client is congenitally difficult.

Your freelancers must remember the simple rule that clients are always right, even when they are wrong. It will help preserve both your relationships with clients and the freelancers' sanity. It also keeps things simple, because it means that everyone who works for you knows where they stand and it eliminates the temptation to fixate on most of the bumps in the road that you encounter.

Your freelancers must remember the simple rule that clients are always right, even when they are wrong.

Put into practice, this approach requires freelancers always to be polite to clients, even if they could cheerfully wring their necks. When faced with problems or snags of any kind, they must always respond constructively and try to come up with helpful solutions.

We do the money

Your freelancers must understand that all discussions about payment rates terms should be with you and all invoices should be addressed to your agency. If they discuss their rates with your clients, the clients will of course know what margin you are making and, if they were so inclined, could insist that you reduced your prices.

It's also important that, other than in exceptional circumstances, rates are agreed with you in advance of work commencing. This is as much down to you as it is to your freelancers. If you don't have a clear agreement in advance, you might be in for a shock when their bill arrives and you see your profit margin go up in smoke.

Freelancers must also keep you up to date on the hours that they have worked and they shouldn't go over those hours without notifying you so that you can confirm the client's agreement. You can't commit to paying overtime that was not agreed as it wouldn't look good if you billed for hours that the client didn't expect to be paying for.

Wave the red flag

If things go wrong and a client is unhappy with your agency's work, you're often the first to know it. Often, but not always. If the freelancer hears of it before you do, it's essential that they report it to you as soon as they are aware of it. That way you can minimise the danger of a little local difficulty escalating in to a crisis.

The same applies if the freelancer thinks they might not hit a deadline. As soon as they feel that is likely, they should inform you so that you can forewarn the client and, if necessary, arrange for a back-up person to step in.

Don't poach

You are operating in a free market and free markets can be brutal. If they were so minded, your freelancers could approach the clients that they have worked for via your agency and offer their services directly, maybe for less than you were charging. There is no law against it, apart from the universal law of *Don't be a Bastard*. To help ensure it doesn't happen, you should spell out to your freelancers that poaching clients is a no-no. Ninety-nine per cent of them will get it and the remaining one per cent you're best rid of.

Don't be a copycat

For a creative freelancer, the fastest route to self-combustion is to plagiarise others' work. The trouble is, if they go up in flames they are likely to burn down your carefully constructed agency. So, whenever you hire someone new, no matter how great their track record, you need to spell it out: *Thou Shalt not Copy!*

Spell out to your freelancers that poaching clients is a no-no. Ninety-nine per cent of them will get it and the remaining one per cent you're best rid of.

MY BIGGEST MISTAKE: LEG 3

WHEN I STARTED WRITE ARM, I DIDN'T BOTHER ESTABLISHING FORMAL RULES FOR THE FREELANCERS WHO WORKED FOR ME. WHILE I TOLD MOST OF THEM A FEW DOS AND DON'TS, I JUST ASSUMED THAT EVERYONE WOULD PLAY BY THE SAME UNWRITTEN RULEBOOK THAT HAD WHEN I WAS FREELANCE. AFTER ALL, THEY WERE ALL RESPONSIBLE PROS.

BUT EVEN THE BEST PEOPLE HAVE BLIND SPOTS. AS THE VOLUME OF WORK INCREASED, SOME OF MY FREELANCERS STRAYED FROM THE STRAIGHT AND NARROW — NOT OFTEN, BUT ENOUGH TO CAUSE ME HEADACHES. FOR EXAMPLE, A COUPLE WERE A BIT SNIPPY WITH CLIENTS AND SOME DISCUSSED THEIR RATES WITH CLIENTS RATHER THAN WITH ME.

EVENTUALLY I ESTABLISHED A SET OF RULES THAT EVERYONE HAD SIGN UP TO. IT DIDN'T COMPLETELY ELIMINATE THE PROBLEMS, BUT IT CERTAINLY KEPT THEM TO A MINIMUM. AND THAT WAS GOOD ENOUGH FOR ME.

LEG
FOUR

10 | A bit of terminology

I work with words and, like many fellow wordsmiths, I'm fairly bad with numbers. Actually, I'm really bad with them. Yet somehow, I managed to build a half-million-pound business. I didn't do so by mastering numbers, I did it by learning enough to get by.

This section is for people like me – creatives who come out in a rash at the sight of a spreadsheet. It won't make you a financial genius, but it will make you good enough and good enough is just fine.

Thankfully, for a KitchenTable agency being good enough with numbers requires far less knowledge than being good enough for a conventional business. This is for the obvious reason that your costs are a lot lower. In particular, you don't have staff so you're not burdened with salaries, pensions, sick pay and the like, and you don't have expensive premises. Also, unlike, say, manufacturing businesses, you don't need to invest in loads of raw materials and equipment.

That said, running a KitchenTable agency isn't like being a

freelancer or still less a staffer. There is quite a lot more you need to know and keep on top of.

Before continuing, you need to grasp the basic terminology of accounting. If you already know it, you can skip this chapter. If you don't, here's a little glossary.

Thankfully, for a KitchenTable agency being good enough with numbers requires far less knowledge than being good enough for a conventional business.

Turnover aka sales aka revenue aka income

This is simply the total value of all your sales minus sales tax (known as VAT in the UK). That's it. Be careful not to confuse it with profits though – you'd be surprised how many people do. If you do, you're knackered.

Cost of sales

This is what each of the items that you sell costs to produce. It only exists if the sale itself exists. Essentially in your case this means the costs of the freelancers you use.

Overheads a.k.a. operating expenses

These are the items that you pay for regardless of whether you make any sales. They might include your telephone, internet and software costs, office rental, computer hardware and any drink and drugs that you consume to cope with the daily workload.

Gross profit

This one's easy – it's your turnover minus your cost of sales. If you don't have a gross profit, you don't really have a business. But you do have a major headache.

Net profit

This is your gross profit minus your overheads. Or expressed another way, your turnover minus your cost of sales and overheads.

If you don't have a gross profit, you don't really have a business.

SIBLING RIVALRY IN THE PROFIT FAMILY

GROSS AND NET PROFIT ARE LIKE SIBLINGS.

GROSS IS THE OLDER, BIGGER ONE WHO FINDS IT EASY TO GET ATTENTION. NET IS THE SMALLER, MORE DIFFICULT ONE WHO IS PRONE TO DISAPPEARING FOR LONG PERIODS.

NET'S EXISTENCE IS ENTIRELY DEPENDENT UPON GROSS, YET, DESPITE ITS SMALLER FRAME, IT IS FAR MORE MUSCULAR THAN GROSS. IT IS THIS MUSCULARITY THAT HAS THE POWER TO MAKE OR BREAK YOU.

TREAT GROSS AND NET WITH EQUAL REVERENCE. NURTURE THEM BOTH AND YOU WON'T GO FAR WRONG. IGNORE THEM AND THEY'LL STICK YOU IN A CONCRETE OVERCOAT AND CHUCK YOU IN THE RIVER.

Cashflow

Cashflow gives you an instant glimpse of your agency's financial health. Put simply, it is the amount of money that goes in and out of your business. What matters though is whether your cashflow is positive or negative.

Positive cashflow means increasing amounts of cash in the bank. It enables you to invest in the business, settle debts, pay expenses and, most importantly, sleep well at night. And negative cashflow? I think you can work that out for yourselves.

Profit & loss: cash v accrual

The profit and loss account (P&L), you won't be surprised to learn, reports on how much money you are making or losing. Typically, it records your turnover, cost of sales, gross profit, overheads and net profit.

You might think accounting is a very rigid discipline, but in truth it can be quite creative – not creative enough to make me want to become an accountant, however. Big businesses can choose from numerous different accounting models, some of the more creative of which have been catastrophic for the business concerned.

For small businesses like ours, the options for the profit and loss account are more limited. The ones that you need to take heed of are the cash method and the accrual method.

Cash accounting is based on cashflow. It records the amounts that go in and out of your bank account. Its value is that it reflects – sometimes brutally – current reality. Its weakness is that it often doesn't tell you how much you are really making or losing.

The accrual method is based on outgoing and incoming invoices. It is a more reliable barometer of the current health of your business, but it can sometimes be divorced from the reality of your bank balance.

CASH V ACCRUAL: A QUICK ILLUSTRATION

IF DURING THE COURSE OF A MONTH YOUR CLIENTS SETTLE INVOICES TOTALLING £10,000 AND YOU SETTLE INVOICES TOTALLING £8,000, THEN UNDER THE CASH METHOD YOU WILL SHOW A £2,000 PROFIT FOR THE MONTH.

IF DURING THAT SAME MONTH YOU ISSUE INVOICES FOR £15,000 AND RECEIVED INVOICES FOR £10,000, THEN UNDER THE ACCRUAL METHOD YOU WILL SHOW A PROFIT OF £5,000.

Balance sheet

The balance sheet is another key indicator of the financial health of a business. If cashflow and P&L are like photos, the balance sheet is like a video of the health of your agency across the years. What it does, essentially, is track a company's assets.

Balance sheets most obviously matter for companies that have large capital assets and liabilities such as premises, equipment, bank loans and stocks of raw materials and finished goods. You might think that for KitchenTable agencies the balance sheet is less important than for, say, manufacturing or retail businesses, for the obvious reason that they don't have large capital assets and liabilities. However, they really do matter for agencies for the simple reason that they record how much you have in the bank. If that amount grows over time, your agency is in good shape. If it diminishes, the agency is in trouble. But, of course, it won't because you'll follow the advice in this book and your business will make you a multi-billionaire.

11 | The basics of financial health

Take care of cashflow

It's a well-worn business cliché: Cash is King. As a writer I try to avoid clichés, so I prefer to say that cash is the Divine Ruler of the Universe, to whom every agency owner – every business owner for that matter – should pray at least ten times a day. Written above her palace gates in huge letters are the words *It's the money in the bank that counts*. Heed them well or you'll be sucked into a black hole never to be seen again.

You might have loads of clients and be doing lots of high value work, but until the money is in the bank, the figures on a page are just that. This matters for two very important reasons.

Firstly, and most importantly, if you don't have money in the bank to pay suppliers they can, if they feel so inclined, make you bankrupt. Many companies have been put out of business by creditors who got fed up with waiting to be paid. So, if your clients don't pay on time, you could conceivably find yourself in the same position. Secondly, without money in the bank you can't invest in the kinds of things you need to make your business grow, like IT, a website upgrade or marketing.

The good news for KitchenTable agency owners is that, unlike many businesses, you are unlikely to have any debtors to whom you owe so much that they could make you bankrupt. You don't have staff, you don't need many – or any – raw materials and you only employ freelancers, most of whom are content to wait a reasonable time to be paid. Nevertheless, you should do all you can to ensure healthy cashflow.

You might have loads of clients and be doing lots of high value work, but until the money is in the bank, the figures on a page are just that.

Watch the overheads

Overheads are a bit like rabbits – turn your back on them for a while and they multiply out of control.

When you start your business, your overheads are likely to be very low. They will be the essentials, like insurance, phone and internet and maybe some basic software subscriptions. But as you expand, they will gradually rack up, to include

THE FIVE GOLDEN RULES OF IMPROVED CASHFLOW

HEALTHY CASHFLOW MEANS ENSURING YOU ARE PAID PROMPTLY, DOESN'T IT? WELL, THERE'S A BIT MORE TO IT THAN THAT. HERE ARE THE FIVE ESSENTIALS

1. BILL CLIENTS IN ADVANCE

MANY CLIENTS WILL BE UNWILLING TO BE BILLED FOR 100% OF YOUR FEE IN ADVANCE, BUT MOST WILL BE FINE WITH 50%.

2. DON'T MAKE YOUR PAYMENT TERMS TOO GENEROUS

YOU'RE A SMALL COMPANY. COMPANIES TYPICALLY INSIST ON BEING PAID WITHIN 28 DAYS, HOWEVER, THERE IS NOTHING WRONG WITH HAVING SHORTER TERMS, INDEED IT'S PERFECTLY ACCEPTABLE TO DEMAND PAYMENT BY RETURN.

3. GENTLY HASSLE LATE PAYERS

SOME ACCOUNTING SOFTWARE SENDS OUT AUTO-REMINDERS, WHICH CAN BE VERY HANDY IF YOU'RE TOO BUSY TO PICK UP THE PHONE.

4. PAY YOUR SUPPLIERS WHEN YOU ARE PAID

MAKE IT CLEAR TO YOUR FREELANCERS THAT FOR CASHFLOW REASON THEY CAN ONLY BE PAID WHEN YOU ARE. OF COURSE, YOU WILL SOMETIMES MAKE EXCEPTIONS FOR WRITERS WHO ARE STRUGGLING FINANCIALLY – YOU'RE A NICE PERSON AFTER ALL.

5. GET YOUR PRICING RIGHT

EVEN IF YOU FOLLOW THE FOUR RULES ABOVE, UNLESS YOU'RE MAKING A DECENT PROFIT, YOUR CASHFLOW WILL BE LOUSY. PROFIT COMES DOWN TO PRICING. TO MAKE A PROFIT YOU NEED TO CALCULATE YOUR COST OF SALES (I.E. YOUR FREELANCER COSTS) ADD SOMETHING TO COVER A SHARE OF YOUR OVERHEADS, THEN ADD ON THE AMOUNT OF PROFIT THAT YOU'D LIKE TO MAKE. FOR MORE PEARLS OF WISDOM ON PRICING, SEE CHAPTER 12.

things like a rented desk space, networking expenses, a telephone answering service and the must-have for all creative business owners (apart from me) a cocaine habit.

For the first few years of Write Arm, I didn't pay much attention to overheads. I knew they were increasing, but when I did the mental arithmetic, they didn't seem too bad. Including the small salary I paid myself,* my desk rental and bookkeeping expenses, I reckoned they amounted to around £1,500 per month.

Then I did the actual arithmetic. I came out in a cold sweat, because the true figure was around £2,500. The list of overheads had grown so long that I could no longer keep them all in my head. Expenses like travel, and subscriptions to various useful organisations and additional software platforms had all failed to make it on to my mental list.

I am not saying that you should not invest in such overheads – in my case they were all vital to the company's success – but I am saying that you should monitor them all in your monthly accounts and always consider their impact on cashflow before extending them.

Overheads are a bit like rabbits – turn your back on them for a while and they multiply out of control.

Check your monthly profit and loss

You know how much money is coming in and going out, don't you? Of course you do, you've made a mental note of

*I paid myself a small salary and made up the rest of my income with dividends.

it all.

The trouble is, your head soon gets full of all the other stuff that piles up when you're running your own business. And when that happens it's easy to get deluded about the state of your finances.

Make sure that, as a minimum, you get a monthly profit and loss (a.k.a. P&L) statement. This will include five key elements: turnover, costs of sales, gross profit, overheads and net profit. Ideally you should have a breakdown of turnover and cost of sales by individual clients and freelance suppliers, although that's not always essential. For the reasons I outlined above, it's far more important to have a breakdown of your overheads, so you can keep tabs on all the different outlays that your agency needs to tick over.

All five figures should be represented as percentages as well as actual amounts. This allows you to see at a glance your gross and net profit margins. In my experience, these are unlikely to be higher than you expected, but they may well be lower. You're only going to improve them if you know what they are in the first place.

The P&L should also provide percentage comparisons with the previous month and, ideally, the same month the previous year. This is vital if you set yourself financial targets. On the subject of which...

Set yourself financial targets

Everywhere you turn in modern life there are targets. Education, health, transport – you name the sector, it's sure to be subjected to our obsession with targets. I always hated target culture and I especially hated it in business. To me it conjured visions of grandmothers being sold by shiny suited sales executives desperate to earn their monthly bonus.

Then I thought again. My agency Write Arm was going nicely, but I had nothing to measure its success against. I lacked direct competitors and, even if I'd had some, they were unlikely to be at the same stage of development as Write Arm. In any case, I wasn't particularly interested in how others were doing.

I realised that the best – perhaps the only – way to measure financial success was to measure the business against some financial targets. Science was with me on this, as numerous studies have shown that those who set targets perform better than they think they can. Why? Because they remove limits on our beliefs about our own abilities.

But what should my targets be? I wasn't chasing super-fast growth as I didn't want to sacrifice my work-life balance. I therefore decided on a reasonably modest growth target of 2.5 per cent per month.

I got my bookkeeper to incorporate the targets, and how I had performed against them, into the monthly P&L. I didn't meet every month's target, but I met most of them and over the course of the financial year I was well ahead.

Having targets is like having a properly thought out and articulated company culture – they are vital coordinates for your journey to world domination.

And, finally, get a good bookkeeper

Of all the evils facing business owners, bookkeeping is the most necessary. If you don't do it, your accounts won't be worth the paper that they're not written on and, if your accounts are worthless, you should get used to drinking cheap alcohol and sleeping in bus shelters, because that's where you'll end up.

Having targets is like having a properly thought out and articulated company culture – they are vital coordinates for your journey to world domination.

But, as with White Lightning cider and Tenants Super lager, creativity and bookkeeping tend not to be a good mix. If you're great at SEO, a wizard coder or a star of PPC then you're probably good at maths, in which case maybe you get a kick out of bookkeeping. But, if you're more the right-brain, creative type then you'd probably rather cut your head off with a penknife than log all your receipts and invoices.

Like brain surgery and bomb disposal, bookkeeping is best left to the experts. It's usually far more difficult than it looks and it takes ages to do. My advice is that it should be a non-fee-earning role that you outsource. If you haven't done it already, you'll be mightily relieved when you do.

Like brain surgery and bomb disposal, bookkeeping is best left to the experts.

CHAPTER

12 | Pricing

What should you charge?

Few questions exercise agency owners more than this one. It looks simple, yet it opens the door to a whole lot of other imponderables, like:

- What profit margin should I make?
- Should I charge by time or by deliverables?
- Should my time be chargeable?
- When should prices be raised?

While there are many easy ways to get your pricing wrong, there is no simple way to get it right. Over the years I learned through trial and error, and from listening to other agency owners, a few basic principles that have served me well. And, yes, I'd like to share them with you.

Start with your desired profit and work backwards

This is a really important exercise to do. I would recommend that you do it, even if you have just started out and are making little or no money, because it gives you the lodestar you need to find your target earnings.

Start by calculating how much you require to live comfortably. You might need to make a list of your basic monthly outgoings, like mortgage or rent, food and fuel bills, vehicle and travel expenses, etc, then multiply the total by twelve.

While there are many easy ways to get your pricing wrong, there is no simple way to get it right.

Next list the non-essential items that you need for a happy life – things like holidays, meals out and crystal meth – and calculate how much you would sensibly spend on them annually.

Add that figure to the essentials total then add ten per cent for unforeseen expenditure, like storm damage repair or accidental pregnancies. Let's say that total comes to £50,000. This is the net amount that you need to take out of the company annually, whether as salary or dividends or, more likely, a combination of the two.

You then need to calculate what profit you would like the

company to make annually on top of what you pay yourself. This, of course, depends on your ambitions and on whether you have plans to invest in, for example, equipment and marketing.

Let's say that figure is £20,000. Add that to your living expenses and you have £70,000. That's the net profit figure you need to aim for, i.e. the profit you make after all your costs of sales, overheads and taxes are paid.

You then divide that figure by the number of days that you work annually. In my case I typically worked around 230 days, so the figure comes to just over £300. So, my daily net profit target was £300 per day.

Next ask yourself how many work projects you can comfortably handle each day. It can be a hard one to answer for three reasons:

1. You might offer a range of services, some of which require more management by you than others.

2. The amount of your time that is required will vary according to where the job is in its life cycle. Typically, if it's in an early phase, it will take more of your time than if it's well established.

3. There will also be times when you can comfortably handle many jobs and other times when you become bogged down in a single one or, worse still, in administrative work that doesn't pay.

So, the answer will probably never be precise and will only come with experience. It's nevertheless a worthwhile exercise.

Pricing

A BIT OF MATHS

SO, YOUR TARGET IS £300 NET PROFIT PER DAY. LET'S SAY THAT YOU CAN TYPICALLY MANAGE THREE PIECES OF ON-GOING WORK PER DAY. THAT MEANS THAT IN ORDER TO HIT THAT TARGET, YOU'LL NEED TO MAKE, YES, YOU GUESSED IT, £100 NET PROFIT FROM EACH OF THEM EACH DAY.

YOU CAN THEN SET YOUR PRICE USING THE FOLLOWING SIMPLE CALCULATION:

COST OF SALE + OVERHEADS + TAX + NET PROFIT MARGIN = AMOUNT CHARGED

SAY YOU HAVE A DESIGN AGENCY AND ARE HIRING OUT FREELANCE DESIGNERS BY THE DAY, YOUR CALCULATION MIGHT RUN AS FOLLOWS:

COST OF SALE (I.E. THE DAILY RATE YOU PAY THE FREELANCERS) = £200

OVERHEADS (THIS WILL BE A HYPOTHECATED FIGURE) = £35

TAX (SAY 10 PER CENT OF GROSS PROFIT) = £15

NET PROFIT = £100

TOTAL DAILY RATE TO CHARGE = £350

EASY. AT LEAST IF YOU A) KNOW HOW MUCH WORK YOU CAN COMFORTABLY HANDLE EACH DAY AND B) WORK ON A SIMPLE PRICING MODEL.

OF COURSE, IT IS LESS EASY IF, LIKE MY AGENCY WRITE ARM, YOU HAD A MUCH MORE VARIED PRICING MODEL, WITH SOME JOBS BEING CHARGED BY THE DAY, OTHERS BY THE PIECE AND WITH RATES VARYING ACCORDING TO THE EXPERTISE OF THE FREELANCERS WHOM YOU USE.

HOWEVER, IF YOU DO CHARGE BY THE PIECE YOU CAN STILL DO SO ON THE BASIS OF A HYPOTHETICAL DAILY RATE, EVEN IF YOU DON'T SHARE THAT RATE WITH YOUR CLIENTS. SO, FOR EXAMPLE, IF WE WERE ASKED TO PRODUCE AN ARTICLE THAT WOULD TAKE THE WRITER HALF A DAY, WE WOULD PAY £100 AND CHARGE £175.

Don't undercharge

Surely this is too obvious to be worth saying. But, hold on, it's not that simple. When you start off and are keen to get work, it's tempting to keep your prices as low as possible and to offer discounts in order to win clients. The temptation is all the more acute if you get off to a quiet start and the phone seldom rings.

My advice is don't do it. There are four reasons:

1. For most clients, low prices are as addictive as heroin. One hit and they're hooked. If any of them become repeat clients, then they will expect low prices every time, which means you're unlikely to make a healthy return on the work you do for them.

2. If they refer you to other clients, those other clients will expect you to work at the same rate and so too will any that they refer you to. And on it goes. Before you know it, you'll be known far and wide as the go-to agency for cheap services.

3. If you charge low prices you can only make money if you sell at high volume. While that's fine for Primark or Walmart, it's not really tenable for a one-person business. Much better that you do a lower volume of higher value jobs.

4. It will, of course, squeeze your margins and knacker your cashflow. I say 'of course' as it seems obvious, but when you're desperate to win clients *the obvious* exits through the same window as sleep, peace of mind and relaxed evenings by the fire.

For most clients, low prices are as addictive as heroin. One hit and they're hooked.

But don't overcharge either

There is a school of thought within the freelance and agency worlds that you should charge whatever you can get away with. 'I think of a number then add a zero,' one freelancer told me, his tongue only halfway in his cheek.

There's one simple reason why you shouldn't overcharge – sooner or later you'll be found out. All it needs is for the person who signs off your bills to be replaced by someone more cost conscious. Before you can say, 'Ok, I'll knock off 50 per cent' you'll find yourself dropped in favour of a cheaper supplier. And, as with undercharging, word will soon get around.

Pricing can, of course, sometimes be guesswork, because you can't always know exactly how much work will be involved in a given job. If you guess that a client will baulk at your quote, you should probably trust your instinct. Before you've been running your agency for very long you will know broadly what you should be charging. You won't always get it right, but you will most of the time. And, unlike brain surgery and bomb disposal, getting it right most of the time is just fine.

There's one simple reason why you shouldn't overcharge – sooner or later you'll be found out.

Work on your margins

Remember, remember, remember, it's your net profit that counts. To remind you, that's the amount left over when you've paid for freelance suppliers *and* your overheads. Your gross margin might be fantastic, but if it's gobbled up by your overheads it's not much use to you.

It's vital to know your net profit margin when calculating your desired profit and your target turnover. I generally aimed for a net profit margin of 15 per cent. If I needed to make £300 net profit per day then, providing I had relatively static overheads, it was relatively easy to set an average daily turnover target.

I would advise that you aim for a similar net profit margin. If it's lower, then you face the same problem as you do with undercharging: you can't make money unless you have a very high volume of work.

Be consistent

Your pricing needs to be consistent. Don't charge one client one rate for a particular service and a very different rate to a similar client for exactly the same service.

Why? You've guessed it, because word will soon get around and you'll lose a lot of credibility and jeopardise your client relationships.

There is some room for manoeuvre, however. A few years ago I modestly increased some of Write Arm's charges. It was no problem for new clients, but one of the most important existing ones resisted and suggested they might consider other suppliers. I decided to keep their rates as they were, but made it clear that they were getting preferential treatment. Importantly, the difference between the old and new rates was not big enough for my new clients to care about, had they learned of it.

But do feel free to vary your rates

Being consistent does not mean that you have to charge all clients the same. In fact, you should actively avoid charging everyone the same. There are two reasons.

Firstly, different suppliers charge different rates, which reflect – or, at least, should reflect – their differing levels of experience and skill. If you are paying different rates, you must charge different rates too. I would charge our copywriters at anything between £200 and £800 per day. Crucially, you must always make clear to clients what, or who, they are getting for their money. If it's someone comparatively junior, then say so, and likewise if they are getting someone very senior.

The second reason is that, in many cases, you should be charging larger clients more. You shouldn't be charging a small start up the same rate that you charge an investment bank. By and large, major corporate clients expect to pay more than smaller ones.

It's worth bearing in mind here that you will generally allocate more senior freelancers to larger clients, so the rates will be higher anyway, but there's still nothing wrong with charging out the same person at different rates, depending upon the size and wealth of the client. Don't take the piss though – adding a zero to your rates will only backfire on you.

MY BIGGEST LEG 4 MISTAKE

BACK IN LATE 2012 WHEN WRITE ARM BEGAN TO PICK UP ITS FIRST SUBSTANTIAL CLIENTS, I DID A STUPID THING, WHICH TOOK THE BUSINESS A LONG TIME TO RECOVER FROQ 1M.

I BEGAN TO PAY ALL OUR FREELANCERS FOR WORK THAT I WAS YET TO BE PAID FOR. WORSE, I PAID THEM AS SOON AS I RECEIVED THEIR INVOICE.

IT WON ME THEIR GRATITUDE, BUT, AS ONE OF THEM DELIGHTEDLY WROTE TO ME, 'THIS ISN'T SUPPOSED TO BE HOW IT WORKS!' I SAID TO MYSELF, 'YES IT IS, I MAKE THE RULES FOR MY OWN BUSINESS AND I TREAT PEOPLE WELL.'

THE TROUBLE IS THAT OUR BIGGEST CLIENT AT THE TIME TOOK WELL OVER 30 DAYS TO PAY. ALTHOUGH I RECEIVED A FAT CHEQUE FROM THEM EVERY MONTH, BY THE TIME IT HIT THE COMPANY BANK ACCOUNT THERE WAS GENERALLY VERY LITTLE IN THERE.

FOR A FEW MONTHS THIS DIDN'T PARTICULARLY WORRY ME, AS THE VOLUME OF WORK WAS INCREASING AND THE FUTURE SEEMED ROSY. BUT WHEN I LOOKED AT THE COMPANY BANK BALANCE IT NEVER SEEMED TO SIGNIFICANTLY INCREASE. WORSE, ALTHOUGH THE MONEY OWING WAS USUALLY ABOUT TWICE AS MUCH AS THAT OWED, THE AMOUNT OWED WAS USUALLY HIGHER THAN THE AMOUNT IN THE BANK.

AT ONE POINT THE AMOUNT OWED WAS OVER 28 TIMES THAT IN THE BANK. I'VE HONESTLY NEVER KNOWN ANY COMPANY WITH SUCH BAD CASHFLOW.

OF COURSE, BY FOLLOWING THE ADVICE I'VE SET OUT EARLIER, I WAS ABLE TO IMPROVE THE SITUATION AND AS I WRITE THAT AMOUNT IS DOWN TO 27 TIMES. (ONLY KIDDING.)

Epilogue: The End and The Beginning

Don't know much about history
Don't know much biology
Don't know much about a science book,
Don't know much about the French I took
But I do know that I love you
And I know that if you love me too
What a wonderful world it would be.

So sang Sam Cook in *Wonderful World*. Replace 'history', 'biology', 'science book' and 'French I took' with 'the digital media', 'marketing', 'running a business' and 'getting clients', then substitute 'I love you' with 'I really do need to make my agency work or I'm f***ed' and replace and 'you love me too' with 'I get it right'.

You now have two things. The first is possibly the worst song of all time – yes, even worse than *The Lady in Red*. The second is an accurate summary of my position when I started my agency, Write Arm. There was a lot more that I didn't know. Terms like SEO and content marketing, which were among the staple activities of my target market, meant nothing to me.

It was no way to start a new business. But then I did it anyway.

If there is one thing above all you need to do, it's take the plunge – even if you haven't nailed down everything in this book. Such advice might horrify some, but don't let your caution put you off.

Remember this one simple fact: greater doubters than you have done it and made a great success of it. So, if they can do it, why can't you? The answer is that there is no reason. Remember, very few people start a business absolutely confident that it will succeed. Almost everyone has doubts and anxieties, even natural risk takers.

If you are not a risk taker, remember that not much is at risk: you're not abandoning your profession and starting again with a blank slate and you're not shelling out money on expensive premises, staff, infrastructure and cocaine. What's the worst that can happen? Bankruptcy, house repossession, divorce, mental breakdown and suicide, that's what. However, it's more likely that you'll be abducted by aliens. The worst that is likely to happen is that you go back to being freelance or a staffer, which isn't too bad is it?

And also remember the benefits that should accrue in the very likely event that your KitchenTable agency is successful: more money, more time, more flexibility and more fun. So, don't wait, get on and do it. You won't regret it. And, if you do, I'll gladly refund you the price of this book. Especially if you got it for free.

Oh, and by the way...

Come and join the KitchenTable Community

Once you've decided to take the plunge, why not join the KitchenTable Community – an online community where agencies form, connect and thrive.

It offers plenty of free content and, if you fancy something deeper, you can do our online course or subscribe for a very modest monthly fee. If you're a subscriber, you'll not only get premium content, but you'll also be able to team up and work with other like-minded agencies and get great deals on a whole range of useful services. Best of all, you'll be part of a supportive club of lovely folk. What's not to like?

Sign up now at Kitchentable.community and turbocharge your agency. You'd be mad not to.

Quiz – Are you ready to start your own agency?

1. Which of these should be a guiding principle of your agency?

> A. What I seek for myself I should also seek for my clients and suppliers
> B. Strive for excellence 24/7
> C. Make money fast and screw everyone else
> D. Principle? What's a principle?

2. How should you communicate your company culture?

> A. Through everything you do and say
> B. On a dedicated page of your website
> C. Print some slogans on beermats and send them to your clients
> D. Tattoo it on your knuckles and brandish your fist in the face of anyone who gets close

3. Which of the following propositions works best for an agency like yours?

A. We are a flexible resource for marketers
B. Websites, branding, marketing, pizza delivery – you name it, we can do it
C. We only want your money
D. Fancy a hook-up tonight?

4. Which are the best types of clients for KitchenTable agencies?

A. i) other agencies and ii) direct clients that are large enough to have a marketing department
B. Any type will do
C. The ones with the deepest pockets
D. Whichever mugs are stupid enough to trust me

5. You have a meeting with the marketing manager of a potential client. Which of the following is likely to win them over?

A. A succinct and easily understood summary of how you can add value to their business and address their pain points
B. A 50-page PowerPoint presentation that details each of your selling points
C. Outrageous flirting
D. A plain brown envelope full of used bank notes

6. You're at a networking event and are having a really good conversation with a new contact. After a few minutes they steer the chat away from business and confess that they're having marital difficulties. Do you:

A. Listen sympathetically and, if appropriate, offer advice
B. Steer the conversation back towards business as soon as possible
C. Start looking around the room for the next person to speak to
D. Give a knowing wink and whisper in their ear that you know a hotel nearby where you can hire rooms by the hour

7. A client complains about the quality of some work that one of your freelancers has delivered. How do you respond?

A. Acknowledge their concern, investigate the matter with the freelancer, then devise a solution that keeps everyone happy
B. Grovel shamelessly until they are pacified
C. Ignore them and hope they will go away
D. Tell them to f*** off and fix the problem themselves

8. A valued freelance supplier is reluctant to work within your client's tight job budget. Do you:

A. Gently negotiate, telling them that you will try to squeeze more money out of the client and promising to put better paid work their way whenever possible

B. End the conversation and look for someone else

C. Tell them they will never work for your agency again

D. Burn their house down – that'll teach 'em!

9. You urgently need to find a niche specialist to work on a client brief, but no one within your current pool of freelancers quite fits the bill: Do you:

A. Put the word out through your existing network and search online resources such as LinkedIn

B. Try one of your regular freelancers and hope that they can handle the brief

C. Buy a book on the subject and have a go and tackling the job yourself

D. Hire an actor

10. A client asks you to quote for a large project of a type that you haven't done before. How should you calculate what to charge?

A. Carefully work out your costs and add a margin that takes into account your management and administration time and leaves you with a reasonable profit

B. Ask around your network of agency owners to see what they would charge

C. Guess and hope for the best

D. Think of the maximum you can charge and add a zero

Results

Mainly As.

Get you – top of the class! You're more than ready to start your own KitchenTable agency. Go forth and do it now.

Mainly Bs.

Not bad, but you need to up your game a little before taking the plunge.

Mainly Cs.

Running a KitchenTable agency probably isn't for you. But, hey, not to worry, you can continue your freelance or staff career.

Mainly Ds.

Get some therapy before we call the cops.

Acknowledgements

Many agency owners and individual creatives have inspired me to write this book and to create the KitchenTable Community. I'm especially grateful to Dan Wardrope of Flexx Digital for first encouraging me in that direction and to my business mentor Si Conroy for his wise guidance at every turn. Daniel de la Cruz, Spencer Gallagher, Peter Hoole, Karl Heasman, Jen le Roux and numerous others kindly shared their wisdom and helped me to hone my thoughts.

My fantastic operations team at Write Arm have allowed me the head space to write the book – a massive thanks to you Rosie and Bryony.

Mat Fidge kindly read my first draft, and David King and Chaz Warriner helped me to proofread the final one. Sam Hudson of Buckley Creative did a great design job and was a model of patience in the face of long delays from my end. Hats off too to Richard Hanson for getting the cover photography spot-on.

Finally, a big thanks to my family and friends for supporting me throughout the journey. I couldn't have done it without you.